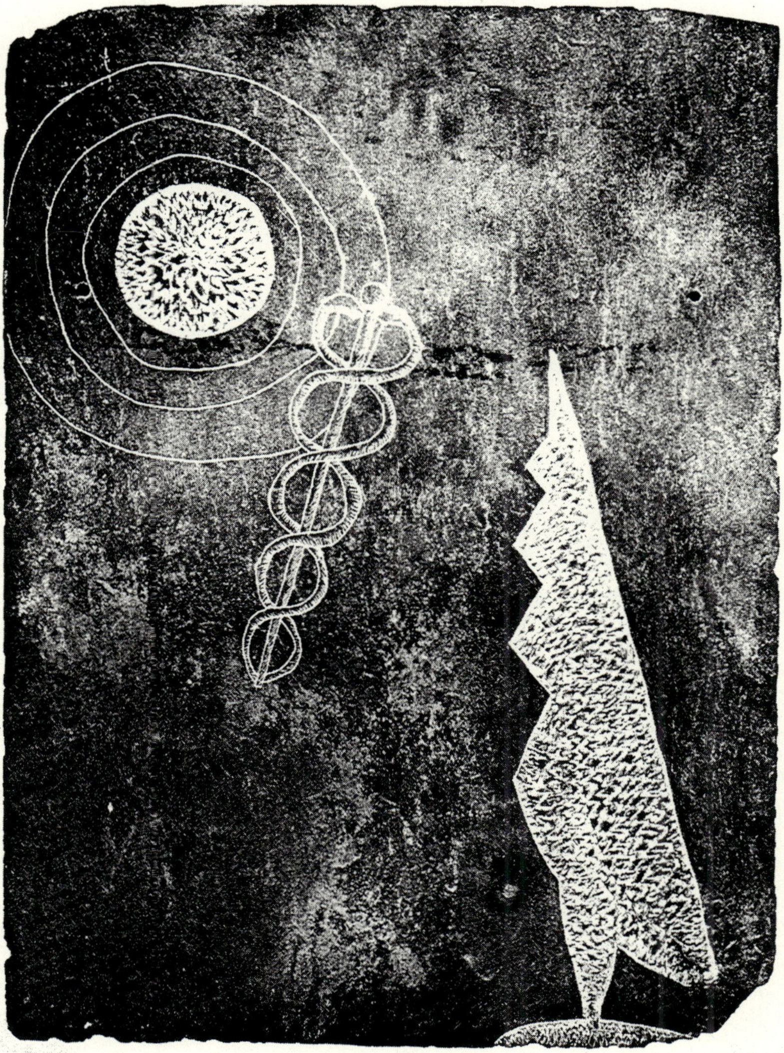

Editorial Inquiries:

Mellen Research University Press
534 Pacific Avenue
San Francisco, California 94133

Order Fulfillment:

The Edwin Mellen Press
Box 450
Lewiston, New York 14092

A COCK FOR ASCLEPIOS
or
Continuing Dialogues
with Socrates, *in extremis*

Francis R. Cronin

EMText
San Francisco

Library of Congress Cataloging-in-Publication Data

Cronin, Francis R.
A cock for Asclepios, or, Continuing dialogues with Socrates, in extremis / Francis R. Cronin.
p. cm.
Includes bibliographical references and index.
ISBN 0-7734-9916-4
1. Plato--Contributions in theory of knowledge. 2. Socrates.
3. Knowledge, Theory of. 4. Love. 5. Logos. 6. Excellence.
I. Title. II. Title: Cock for Asclepios. III. Title: continuing dialogues with Socrates, in extremis.
B398.KC76 1991
184--dc20 91-3331
CIP

Editorial Inquiries:

Mellen Research University Press
534 Pacific Avenue
San Francisco
CA 94133

Order Fulfillment:

The Edwin Mellen Press
P.O. Box 450
Lewiston, NY 14092
USA

Printed in the United States of America

for Janet

TABLE OF CONTENTS

PREFACE

Socrates *in extremis,* yes, but also Western Culture *in extremis.*

The heart of the following is an interpretative recollection of the dialogue that occurred in Socrates' cell on the last day of his life. Truly, Socrates was during that dialogue *in extremis.*

In the eyes of not a few of our contemporaries, Western Civilization today is *in extremis.* It is headed down a path of self-destruction, the outcome of which, at best, will be its relinquishing its position of dominance in the world or, at worse, the annihilation of human life on the planet Earth.

The thesis of the work is that Socrates *in extremis* just might have something valuable, even something salvational, to say to Western Civilization *in extremis.*

A Cock for Asclepios is not meant to be yet another scholarly interpretation of Socrates-Plato. It is not a scholarly interpretation at all.

Scholarly interpretations operate within accepted parameters of normal discourse, and comport themselves according to accepted norms of information-collection and argumentation.

A Cock for Asclepios challenges the accepted norms that have governed at least our Modern (16-19 cent.) interpretation of Plato. It does not, however, argue-down traditional interpretations, nor does it contend with twentieth-century 'deviant' interpretations, some of which are not too removed from itself and to many of which it is indebted.

Rather, *A Cock for Asclepios* is a radical reinterpretation of Socrates-Plato, and a questioning of the advisability of applying the 'medicaments' to current ailments, the curative effectiveness of which prompted Socrates long ago to command Criton to pay a cock to Asclepios.

F.R.C.

ACKNOWLEDGMENT

My own indebtedness is legion. Because this work emerges from my first year classes in Philosophy, I want to thank the many St. Thomas University students who put up with me over the years and who challenged me to better focus my criticism and reinterpretation.

To my colleagues for your comments and support, especially professors A. Bentley, F. Burke and Dr. B. MacLean, thank you; and to professor Jim Asher without whose dedication of time and editorial attention this book never would have seen the light of day,thank you.

To my own professors at Saint Mary's and Fordham Universities, and especially to Dr. James M. Somerville who not only directed my early study of Greek Philosophy, but also encouraged me throughout the long gestation of this work, thank you.

To our children, who for years were jealous of the fact that Daddy was allowed every day to play with "play-dough", a very special thank you.

And finally, I herewith acknowledge with gratitude financial assistance towards manuscript preparation contributed by St. Thomas University.

Whatever of value there might be in this book, I owe to you all and others not mentioned. The inadequacies alone are my own fabrication and responsibility.

INTRODUCTION

> Concerning life, the wisest men of all ages have judged alike: It is no good. Always and everywhere one has heard the same sound from their mouths—a sound full of doubt, full of melancholy, full of weariness of life, full of resistance to life. Even Socrates said, as he died: "To live—that means to be sick a long time: I owe Asclepios the Savior a rooster. " Even Socrates was tired of it.
>
> Friedrich Nietzsche,
> *Twilight of the Idols*
> #44, I.

This is not a work on Nietzsche. I chose to preface this study of Socrates and Plato with these words of his, not because I consider him an excellent guide to the intricacies of Platonic thinking—though, in spite of himself, I can think of few better than he—but because this particular quotation articulates rather nicely the perennial impact that Platonic Philosophy has had on Western culture, and precisely the impact which I will herein try to dissipate.

Traditionally, Plato has conveyed to subsequent generations and cultures a message of substantial dualism. There is a wide chasm separating Being and Becoming, Soul and Body, Spirit and Matter. We humans are confused creatures, half spirit and half matter, fated to live out our earthly lives in this region of matter until we can return to our rightful home in the intelligible heavens after death.

Quite apart from the fact that there is no real basis for such an interpretation in the dialogues, the danger of this interpretation lies in our turning away from Plato and turning a deaf ear to his message. Few today, and rightly so, would devote much attention to such life-weariness and this-worldly-pessimism as Nietzsche's Socrates advocates. And even if we are to enter a prolonged period of industrial and technological decline, as some environmentalists are already announcing, such dualistic blatherings would be no adequate response at all.

No, Nietzsche is right. Let us have nothing to do with the melancholy and weariness of *such* a Socrates.

But what if Socrates and Plato were singing an entirely different tune? What if Socrates and Plato were actually battling dualism and its attendant melancholy and weariness? What if Plato, especially, was struggling with the very meaning of human life itself in an effort to delineate the orientation and pattern of human excellence? Would we listen then?

Willy-nilly, each and every one of us has listened to Plato. He is indelibly stamped on each of our souls, for he is the crucible and well-spring of our Western culture. Far more perhaps than any of us are willing or able to admit, Plato colors our Western destiny.

One does not easily extricate oneself from one's heritage, even when, like ours, it seems to be headed down an environmental and demographic *cul-de-sac*. But it is possible to reassess it, especially when the dominant voice coloring one's self-interpretation is today heard to be singing a different tune than previously.

Plato is that dominant voice, and today, and for much of the current century, he is heard to be singing quite a different tune than he sang for our forebearers.

Plato lived in the fourth century B.C. Athens, during the declining years of her "golden age". He saw her culture and her empire collapse, and he passionately strove to erect a new culture, a new model of human excellence, the pursuit of which might extricate civilization from the confusion and disasters into which it was then falling. Plato strove to create a model of rational or *logical* excellence as befitting man. This last word is important, for the record of human history, and not only Western, is the record of (male!) man playing god or beast, but by all means refusing to play the role of man as man, of human being precisely as human being.

Do not consider it an easy role to play man as man. And do not consider it an easy task to discover an appropriate model of human excellence. In culturally homogeneous times, the problem is perhaps not so onerous—one simply follows tradition. But what does one do when homogeneity gives way to heterogeneity and when traditions compete with each other? And what does one do when the traditions to which one has access one and all prove unsatisfactory and even destructive?

Such was precisely Plato's situation in ancient Athens. And such is perhaps our own situation today. Plato fashioned a model of human excellence which succeeding generations refused to attend to or to follow, but which might prove opportune and even viable for us today.

Anyway, that is what this book is all about. It is an elaboration of Plato's model of human excellence, and an investigation, albeit abstractly, of its applicability today. It is a meditation, a very personal and probably overly-imagistic meditation, on Socratic *not*-knowing, and its contention is that Plato develops a pattern of human rationality as *erotic-hypothesizing*.

Plato is the creator of the hypothetical method, and whereas we make a great fuss about its empirico-scientific application, very few of us have the courage to apply it to the full extent of our cultures and institutions. Plato did.

Erotic-hypothesizing means that we don't know. It means that we know that we don't know, and that on the basis of this knowing that we don't know we rouse ourselves to try to find out. We rouse ourselves to know. But we will fail. We will never succeed. Pessimism? On the very contrary—perhaps it is the only knowing available to human beings. It is, finally, optimistic, *humanly* optimistic.

The following work, then, is an effort to delineate human *not*-knowing in the Platonic dialogues.

The title of the book, of course, recalls Nietzsche's statement with which I began this Introduction. I chose this particular statement of his because of the title of this work which I had previously chosen, and not the other way around. It will be readily apparent to you as you read the work, and especially my interpretation of the *Phaedo* itself, that I completely disagree with Nietzsche's interpretation of Socrates' last command or statement. But this involves me already in erotic-hypothesizing.

Erotic-hypothesizing is reflexive; it rebounds on itself. I do not claim by any stretch of the imagination that this is *the* definitive interpretation of Plato. I hope I am on target, however, but I'm sure that anything of value I do say could be said much more nicely and beautifully. And more's the pity for that, because beauty, we think, is an effulgence of the Good which calls us above ourselves in the unending pursuit of excellence.

It is up to others to do better.

On the one hand, in the following work I want to argue very strenuously that this "yet another interpretation of Plato" needs no justification. An interpretation must be "substantiated", "shown to fit the facts", yes. But an interpretation never needs to be *justified* in the sense of apologizing for its fabrication in the first place. We humans are inveterate interpreters. We are condemned to interpretation even as, *pace* Jean-Paul Sartre, we are condemned to freedom.

On the other hand, I know full-well that an interpretation of Plato, and especially one that dubs itself a "new" interpretation, indeed calls for justification, at least to the extent that some apology must be offered for directing attention at him rather than at a more contemporary thinker.

Alfred North Whitehead some time ago claimed that the whole history of Western philosophy is but a series of footnotes to Plato. But this is to claim that Western *culture*—understanding philosophy to be but the self-conscious and self-reflective dimension of culture—is but a series of footnotes to Plato. Be this as it may, and there are many critics and students of "culture" who buy it, "footnotedness" does not of itself justify our turning our attention to the "text", and in this case all the way back to the dialogues of Plato.

I agree, provided the footnotes are satisfactory and give us no trouble. But if such is not the case, if the footnotes prove to be cumbersome and unintelligible (and unviable!), we must turn to the text itself if we want to understand the footnotes at all.

Now the point of all this is that we have no option but to understand and grapple with the footnotes in question. The footnotes, after all, are our culture, our learned behavior, our learned way of dealing with the world. And if our dealings with the world backfire and break down we have no option but to tinker with these very dealings themselves.

But have our learned ways of dealing with the world broken down? Opinion is divided on this score between what we can refer to as the Optimists and the Pessimists. The Optimists want more of the same: "batten down the hatches, full steam ahead!" is their motto. Jobs and technology, more and bigger and better will see us through. Especially technology, for technology will solve all the problems which the Pessimists keep throwing up to us.

The Pessimists, on the other hand, speak of environmental pollution, nuclear annihilation, over-population, exploitation and unemployment. If one has a short-term attention span and lends even half an ear to current news coverage, it is difficult not to side with the Pessimists. And even if one is gifted with a long-term attention span, the Pascalean imbalance of the consequences tends to nudge one towards their side. After all, acid rain and the potential destruction of the forests of the earth, water pollution and the potential death of the oceans, nuclear radiation and the potential spoiliation of the soil for hundreds of thousands of years are no light-weight consequences. We are facing, the Pessimists tell us, nothing less than the destruction of life on the planet Earth.

It is all too easy to shut our ears to both camps.

But what if the Pessimists—for they are undeniably the more startling—are right? It might be a small irritant which starts me thinking: am I wrong, or does it really seem to be the case that there have been more fish-kills lately? Why is the maple-sugar production declining so precipitously in eastern North America? Are viral infections hanging on a little longer nowadays?

But I don't believe the Pessimists are right. And, damn it all, even if I thought they were right, I wouldn't simply throw in the towel anyway. No, the only viable option open to us is a judicious mingling of the two, a judicious mingling of the Optimistic and the Pessimistic claims.

I sometimes imagine Western Civilization as on board a train speeding towards a precipice. We Westerners cannot escape the train, our cultural container, and yet we know that we are heading towards disaster. Increasing our speed, "more of the same", will but hasten the end. It is imperative that we slow our forward advance, and steer a new course away from the precipice looming ahead.

But I haven't finished outlining my metaphor yet. You see, not only are we on board a speeding train, but the forward locomotives pulling the train are sealed off. We cannot get at the controls and steering mechanisms in them.

We are hurtling towards our fateful destiny, and there is absolutely nothing we can do about it. And so we distract ourselves. We watch our t.v. soaps, game-shows, and sit-coms. We drink our beer, and we exercise; oh yes, we exercise frantically in our various "participaction" programs. And withal, we are pushed and prodded, organized and regimented.

Finally, perhaps, someone asks what is at the back of the train. If the front is sealed off, perhaps the back is open, and perhaps there is something of interest and importance there. Then this Socrates amongst us, joined hopefully by a few like-minded and inquisitive souls, wends his way to the back of the train only to discover that the train is *pushed* as well as pulled, and that the mechanism which controls the speed and direction of the train is at last partially accessible from the rear locomotive.

This perhaps far-fetched metaphor operates within the context of a declining cultural vitality. When an individual or a society is alive and enthusiastic, (s)he and they are pulled eagerly into the future by the very attractiveness of the future itself. (S)he and they enthusiastically command the lead locomotive and steer the train into the options which lie ahead, which the future itself presents. But when enthusiasm wanes we are banished from active leadership, and we discover ourselves—in our case—thrown into a hurtling projectile the very momentum of which frightens us.

The philosopher John Macmurray tells us that "philosophy is necessary when religion fails." That is to say, an interpretative re-evaluation of ourselves is necessary when our culture fails and our enthusiasm wanes. In the context of our train metaphor, at such a time we must retreat (pessimistically) to the back of the train so that therefrom we might once again grasp the controls (optimistically) and steer a more responsible and cooperative course into a viable future.

Now it is not yet clear what any reinterpretation of Plato has to do with all of this, and especially with this silly metaphor! Are we going to find Plato, for crying-out-loud, in the rear locomotive somehow capable of assuming control of our destruction-bound train? After a manner of speaking, that is exactly what I am suggesting. But I am far from being a necrophile, and I do not imagine any exhumation of Plato or simplistic return to the past. As I recall, Plato's dabblings in politics in his own lifetime came to naught, and I see no reason why we should expect anything different today were "philosophers to become kings or kings become philosophers".

Let me board my metaphor again. I agree with the Whiteheadean statement that Plato, in effect, is the well-spring of our Western cultural tradition. Plato is the "Casey Jones" who has driven our Western train these past two thousand plus years, and in the last three hundred years, unerringly and with increasing momentum towards self-destruction. And now this mad engineer sits sealed into his forward compartment beyond our reach. We cannot talk to him, and most of us have forgotten that he even exists.

But here's the clincher. Plato does *not* sit in the front compartment! He sits rather in the rear. But this is not correct either.

Plato sits nowhere. He is dead. Rather his "spirit" sits in the front *and* in the rear compartments, and the 'Plato' who sits in the rear and is accessible to us is quite a different character from the 'Plato' who sits in the front.

And now it is time to put my metaphor to rest. Let me retire my train and my engineers and admit, simply, that what drives our culture, what drives any culture, are the suppositions that animate it, the assumptions and suppositions that have been handed down through history and still direct its trajectory. Suppositions are operative only to the extent that they are understood by a people, and they are understandingly handed on to a people. *Suppositions,* therefore, *are very much within out understanding, and within our interpretative power.*

What, then, are the suppositions which feed our Western culture, which fuel our Western tradition which has blossomed into the dire predicament in which we today find ourselves? (Here I'm siding with the Pessimists.)

Western history is far from having been a continuous process of development. Continuity prevailed, yes, but it has been spiced with discontinuity, the most significant of which perhaps was the Industrial Revolution. In a very real sense, we are today reaping the harvest that was sown some three hundred years ago with the emergence of the Industrial Revolution in England. And the issue of this Industrial Revolution? Technology.

The industrial revolution itself is implicated within the two hundred years older Renaissance, and which must itself be seen as a negative reaction to—and thereby controlled by—the mediaeval "sacramentalism" which preceded it. And the fruit of the Renaissance? Individualism.

Technological-individualism is the heart of the predicament in which we find ourselves today. Technological-individualism is the significant discontinuity which distinguishes us from our predecessors. It is the very success of our twentieth-century technological-individualism which has gotten us into the mess in which we now find ourselves. Our automobiles and urban comforts have cut us off from and polluted the natural environment. Our health-delivery systems and demographic proliferation have cut us off from our neighbors. Our defense systems have so successfully protected us from enemy aggression that we now face the specter of nuclear annihilation. And our manufacturing plants and energy-producing systems are so successful that we are almost drowning in products and waste.

In the words of Martin Heidegger, "enframing" reigns, and everyone and everything is relegated increasingly to "standing reserve".

But lying beneath and sustaining this discontinuity is a strata of continuity which alone makes the discontinuity possible, and which we must uncover if we wish to understand ourselves and understand the situation in which we now find ourselves.

Dualism, *substantial*-dualism, grounds the technological-individualism which so characterizes our modern Western culture. Indeed, substantial-dualism grounds the whole of our Western culture and tradition. It is the continuity that grounds and underlies the more sensational discontinuities which grab our attention. And for all the attention devoted to the latter, it is the former, the underlying continuity, which is the most important and the most "substantial".

But what has any of this to do with Plato? And what possibly, given the overwhelming force of the momentum and trajectories at play, could a simple reinterpretation of Plato effect anyway?

To address the first question, it has everything to do with Plato, for *substantial-dualism is our Platonic legacy.*

Technological-individualism can operate only in a field that is devoid of standing values and structures which demand that they be taken into account. Technological-individualism can be played only on a "level playing field". Such a level field is the other side of the Platonic coin which is our legacy.

We do not usually recognize this because we concentrate on Plato's dualism. Plato divided the world into being and becoming, into spirit and matter, into soul and body. He divided the human world into two "worlds", the world of biologic and economic transactions which occupy our day-to-day interests, and the world of spiritual values and intelligible truths which occupy our specifically human minds and souls. At best, the first is but a means to and reminder of the second, for humanity's true home lies not on this earth, but in the world of being which will be the philosopher's lot after death. Christianity, encouraged perhaps by the severity of life in the ancient and mediaeval worlds, lapped-up this dualism, and directed our attention to life-after-death and its contrasting but equally eternal rewards.

The consequence of this was that this world of spatio-temporal existence was rendered unintelligible and sterile, a level and plain field within which we could play as we desired and within which we could move as we were able.

For centuries we were able to do very little and so little damage was done, and the precariousness of our dualistic culture did not reveal itself. Such is not the situation today, however, and yet the habits formed in the last two thousand years, and especially in the last three hundred, render us almost completely impotent with respect to altering our momentum and changing our patterns of behavior.

But what, even if such is realistically possible, could a mere reinterpretation of Plato effect? I honestly don't know. Perhaps nothing at all. On the other hand, perhaps a *viable* reinterpretation of

Plato could prepare us to reassess our patterns of behavior, given the difficulties that our traditional patterns are encountering today.

Alteration of behavioral patterns requires two motivating factors: a negative blockage of traditional patterns, and a positive appreciation that change is possible and a particular change desirable. The news today is filled with recurrent and newly emerging blockages to our traditional ways of "conducting business". Negativities abound. It is my hope that a reinterpretation of Plato, perhaps along the lines I here advocate, will contribute to the positive motivation we so desperately need.

Much more than we recognize, human beings are *responsive* creatures. We respond to stimuli in our environment and in our cultural milieu. We respond to obstructions that block us by shunning them. We respond to opportunities that open before us by pursuing them. The resulting dance, responding to the negative and positive stimuli constantly challenging us, is our human life, individual as well as collective. Let me now describe some of the stimuli which have influenced my response to Plato.

This interpretation arises out of my Freshman courses in philosophy over the past twenty-five years of college-level teaching. Initially, I presented Plato to my students after the manner in which he was presented to me as an undergraduate student in the late fifties, hewing rather closely to the typical History-of-Greek-Philosophy-textbook version. The initial change I made with my own classes—and it did not strike me as being momentous at the time—was that I used Plato's dialogues (in translation) as the class text rather than the formal, and sometimes historical, textbooks to which I had been subjected.

At the same time I was reading widely among twentieth-century commentators, and gradually became convinced of the importance of Plato's artistic achievements and the concomitant importance of attending to the dramatic settings and nuances he inserted in his dialogues. Somehow, and in a manner then unclear to me, I adopted the conviction that the settings and the incidental remarks and exchanges passing between the characters were important, and inextricably involved in the very philosophical message that Plato was trying to convey to us through the dialogues.

It was the *Phaedo* which first bothered me, and gradually effected a break in the dike that I, following what I thought was the traditional interpretation of Plato, had erected. Rather quickly the original trickle dribbling through gave way to a roaring flood, in the midst of which I'm still trying to gain my sea legs.

It was the blatant *dualism* of the *Phaedo* that first tripped me up. Of course, and as I myself had been taught, I waxed poetically on the *Phaedo*'s distinction between the soul and the body, on the manifest superiority of the soul and its thinking to the body and its sensing. I taught and elaborated the various demonstrations of psychic and personal immortality, and emphasized our responsibility to separate our soul from our bodies as far as we can in this life so that we could understand the better, and thus be assured that we would be rewarded in the intelligible and spiritual heaven of the after-life.

All the while I was becoming increasingly attuned to the role of "cultural model" in which Plato had cast Socrates. Socrates, a veritable "man for all seasons", was being thrown up before us for emulation. He was the new hero, almost a savior, the imitation of whom would lead us into the spiritual path of Philosophy and the eternal rewards of the next life. Of course I ignored the "great year" and reincarnation as being entirely too mythical and too deviant from our Christian tradition and truth.

And then, horror of horrors, the dramatic setting of Xanthippe and her sons hit me. Not only does Plato mention Socrates' sexuality and reproductive prowess in an early scene in the dialogue—in the very first scene in which Socrates appears, he is accompanied by his wife and infant son—but towards the end, in the second last scene of the dialogue, he again mentions his wife, and seems to go out of his way to announce that Socrates has *three* sons, you know. What is going on here? What is the point of all this? The most dualistic and even *anti* body and *anti* matter of all the dialogues dramatically *emphasizes* the fact that Socrates is a very bodily, a very material, even a very sexual individual! Was dualism, at least understood along traditional and substantial lines, *not* the message of the *Phaedo*? Was the personal immortality of the human soul *not* the central issue in the *Phaedo*?

I continued to read the dialogue, but now paid much closer attention to the dramatic nuances scattered throughout it. I focused on the philosophers' "practicing dying" and on Socrates' rejoinder to Simmias that no one had yet discovered "in what sense the real philosophers wish to die and deserve to die, and what kind of death it is." This seemed to indicate that the "death" in question might not be physical or normal death, as it has been invariably interpreted in our tradition, and that perhaps something quite different was at issue here.

And then I looked at Socrates' last words. I thought it significant that Plato dramatically recorded these last words, and I wondered, both in the context of the *Phaedo*, as well as in the context of the other dialogues, what "Criton we owe a cock to Asclepios" could possibly mean.

By this time, of course, I had long since discarded (one of) the traditional interpretations that Socrates was rewarding Asclepios for healing his soul from its life-long sickly affiliation with his body. And I was no longer happy that Plato's message had anything to do, centrally at least, with personal immortality anyway.

Asclepios was the god of healing. It would seem reasonable, then, that a debt owed to Asclepios was incurred because a healing had taken place, and this healing was (or could be) attributed to Asclepios. Is there, then, any reference to a disease, and to a healing from this disease, in the dialogue? But as soon as we ask the question, the answer jumps forth: Yes; one disease is particularly emphasized at the beginning of Socrates' autobiographical excursion, and the healing from this disease is indicated at the end of it. *Misology* is the "worst disease which can befall man," and Socrates' *Logos* or "second voyage in search of a cause" effects the healing therefrom.

All of which, of course, highlighted Socrates' autobiographical excursion. I was now laying increasing emphasis on this peculiarly parenthesized scene in the dialogue. It is the only scene quite so singularly emphasized in the whole of Plato's writings, and more and more I perceived it as being not so much a biographical account as being, rather, a delineation of the new pattern of thinking that is the central message of the *Phaedo*. Therein Socrates recounts his own break with cosmological and natural-philosophical thinking and delineates his own and new pattern of thinking, his own and new excursion into *Logos*-thinking, as being the new model of human excellence.

Anyway, it was this delineation which elicited the enigmatic declaration of healing from Echecrates, and which justifies Socrates' last words that he owes a debt to Asclepios because, indeed, a healing had taken place.

This was my touchstone, my home base, and proceeding from here I read the other dialogues as being Plato's presentation of Socrates as modelling, in various roles and situations, a new image of *Logos* and a new image of what it is to be a human being as the *logical* animal.

Socrates appeared to me as a cultural hero exemplifying, and a cultural force advocating, the transformation of human nature. He contended with traditional models of human excellence, and opposed most sharply alternative depictions of excellence then vying for model-status. Persistently and consistently, I saw Plato presenting Socrates to us as *the* model of human excellence, and as a "savior" from the troubles besetting us.

And this brings me to the positive stimuli which have influenced my interpretation.

Let me at the very beginning set aside the plethora of excellent Platonic scholarship flourishing today. I have learned a great deal from much of it, but, almost without exception, at bottom it has impacted on me as a "preaching to the converted". Reading contemporary scholars—and I do not pretend to scholarship after their manner—has helped me to polish my arguments, sharpen my perception, and pick up on nuances and refinements I might otherwise have missed. But the central positive stimulus in my interpretation has been my own Christian heritage and tradition.

Here I must be careful, for I claim at the same time that our Christian tradition has grossly misinterpreted Plato (and done itself major damage in the process). There are two points of the Christian tradition which are important to my philosophical purpose: humanity is created by a loving creator, i.e., and stated less theologically, humanity is implicated within a good and intelligible whole which is greater than it is; and two, this whole draws humanity towards itself.

Not surprisingly, the allegory of the Cave plays an important role in my understanding of Plato.

I do not deny that the *Republic* has given me more difficulty than any other of the middle-period dialogues. Even reading it as an epistemological/psychological treatise rather than as a political/-sociological treatise has not immuned me to the absolutism and the all-too-pure-cleanliness of many of its pronouncements.

It might be the absence of just such cleanliness from the three allegories which initially attracted me to them. Socrates had built-up the dramatic tension to the point that it was admitted that only one who clearly perceived the good could rule the *polis*/soul. But when challenged to say what the good is he begs off claiming he does not know, and offers instead three allegories or metaphors, each of which is blatantly tentative and filled more with not-knowing than with knowing.

Of the three, the allegory of the Line is the most descriptive methodologically, and the only one, by the way, which is introduced by Socrates with the words that he "will not now willingly leave anything out if (he) can help it." The allegory of the Sun strikes me as peculiarly cosmological and substantial—at least this is how it has been interpreted in our tradition; I will qualify my own interpretation below in the text. The Cave is a pointedly existential allegory and is introduced, I believe, as a pictorial representation and elucidation of the Line.

While the Cave is central to my interpretation of Plato, I cannot emphasize too strongly that it is the Cave as an existential representation of the Line which plays this role. It is decidedly *not* the Cave as depicting any type of substantial dualism or two-world dichotomy, and which, of course, has been its dominant interpretation in our tradition.

The Cave, then. What strikes me as most important in this allegory is the *light* which penetrates to the very depths of the cave, casts (i.e., grounds) the shadows on the back wall, and is yet invisible to the prisoners. The unarticulated heart of this allegory is that it is the light which simultaneously penetrates the cave and calls the prisoners forth, and yet this same light hides itself in illuminating the objects seen and attended to. Indeed, the more the objects are attended to, the less possibility there is of ever attending to the light. Finally, the *integrity* of this allegory attracts me. The escaped and now enlightened prisoner returns to the cave to lead the others forth. Never mind that none follow him and he is, depicting the fate of Socrates, rewarded with death for his efforts. What is important is that the human excellence represented in this allegory consists in an integration of soul and body, of thinking and acting. It consists in the intelligent organization of practical living, regardless of the fact that any definitive understanding of reality remains forever beyond our human grasp—these are allegories, remember, not the apodictic definition that was originally requested of Socrates.

It is almost as if centuries ago Plato, too, was suggesting that "a man's reach should exceed his grasp". I doubt that he would have followed it up with Browning's "or what's a heaven for". No, I imagine rather he would have claimed that it is precisely the ungraspableness of that for which we reach which alone prompts us to reach out in the first place. Most certainly something like this operates in the *Symposium*, and without it, the Socratic claim to not-know is nonsensical.

I remember reading somewhere that indeed Socrates' claim to not-know *was* nonsense. He knew; he just wouldn't tell us. I shall argue below that such a claim itself is nonsense. Moreover, I think it can be demonstrated that this nonsensical claim, appropriately modified to fit into Christian dress, has, in truth, been the prevailing supposition of our Western cultural tradition. That is to say, it is not so much Socrates who knew as it is we Christians who know, we pious recipients of divine revelation who know and are burdened with the responsibility of "sharing" this knowledge with our less fortunate brethren.

Now if this, even possibly, is the prevailing supposition that animates our cultural tradition, what would happen if we were to entertain the opposite supposition *that we don't know*, that no one ever knows absolutely? Would not such a supposition if ever adopted "turn life upside down?" And, of course, this was exactly the consequence predicted by Callicles (in the *Gorgias*) if what Socrates said were true!

If we wish to remain even minimally faithful to the philosophy of Plato as described in the dialogues preserved in our tradition, we have no option but to recognize that *Socrates did not know,* and that the model of human excellence depicted in the person and behavior of Socrates entails that *human beings do not know;* that in the very heart of (human) knowing lies not-knowing.

And this not-knowing lying at the very center of knowing is not an emptiness that can ever be filled. Along that path lies the self-righteousness and arrogance that killed Socrates. No, human nature is not the sufficient one. Noetically and ontologically human nature is insufficient and incomplete. And it is only in full recognition of this deficiency that we can ever truly love (*Eros*) and truly know (*Logos*), which, after all, is what Socrates and Plato and Christianity are all about anyway.

The second positive stimulus influencing my interpretation of Plato is the very pervasiveness of interpretation itself today, and the growing awareness of the role that interpretation plays in our lives.

Perhaps it is the effectiveness of the Pessimists' propaganda which is nudging us into taking a "second look" at our own actions. Perhaps it is the difficulties we are encountering that prompt us to look at how other cultures and peoples behave to ascertain what, if anything, they have going for them. Undoubtedly, the increase in communications and travel is pertinent. But for whatever reasons, increasingly we have become aware that "ours is not the only game in town".

On a more philosophical note, it is not at all surprising that respect for interpretation and the role of interpretation should prevail today. For while existential-phenomenology has crested as an intellectual fad, its "perspectivism", "contextualism" and "knower-implicated-within-the-known" remain very much with us. Sociology-of-knowledge, in its various guises, has extended the philosophical proclamation into wider fields. Psychology emphasizes the phenomenon of "projection". And the mutual implication of knower and known is very much present even in the more natural and strict sciences of Physics and Mathematics.

On the one hand, none of this should be taken as denying the existence among us of antiquarian absolutists. "Fundamentalists" of various persuasions abound, but increasingly, I hope, they are seen to be narrow and fearful claimants-to-infallibility rather than the paragons of virtue that they say they are.

On the other hand, sheer relativism is quite unacceptable. Interpretation must respond to the facts it purports to interpret. Second, interpretation must self-consciously be aware of its conditions and suppositions, both those 'externally'-motivated by the culture and times within which it operates and those more 'internally'-motivated by the philosophical and religious forces acting upon it.

Thus far, albeit perhaps inadequately, I have discussed the 'external' and the 'internal'-religious stimuli acting on my interpretation of Plato. Let me conclude this Introduction with a few remarks on the 'internal'-philosophical stimuli acting on it.

So far as I can now see, Nietzsche and Heidegger are the two philosophers who have most influenced my reading of Plato. But this is not at all to say that I agree with their interpretations of him. Most emphatically I do not.

From Nietzsche I've acquired my comfort with the interpretative model, and my relaxation with the realization that cultures are existentially-motivated and value-laden interpretations designed to further a course of life. And from him also, perhaps, I've picked up a realization that, because "god is dead", there is no external authority which can pronounce an interpretation right or wrong, true or false. Inevitably, we grope around in the murky waters in which we swim and make the most of it.

Heidegger's influence on me is more pervasive, I think. I am captivated by his image of human reality as *Da-sein*, as the here/there of the revelation of Being. I also enjoy his insistence on *Dasein*'s *responding* to the self-presencing of re-velation, in opposition to any subjective or anthropological projection of intelligibility and value.

How much my indebtedness to either might have contributed to a misinterpretation rather than a reinterpretation of Plato the reader will have to decide for her/himself.

The body of the work consists of separate interpretations of selected dialogues from Plato's middle-period. There are interpretations of the *Apology*, the *Meno*, the *Phaedo*, the *Symposium* and sections of the *Republic*. A unifying theme runs throughout these interpretations, but they were written separately and little effort has been made to disguise the fact.

In the concluding Interpretation I will tie them all together, and try to articulate, clearly and concisely, Plato's middle-period message to his contemporaries then, but especially to us now.

And finally, let me let the cat out of the bag and tell you, in Plato's own words, where all this is going:

> Then supposing you should ever hence-forth try to conceive afresh, Theaetetus, if you succeed, your embryo thoughts will be better as a consequence of today's scrutiny, and if you remain barren, you will be gentler and more agreeable to your companions, having the good sense not to fancy you know what you do not know.
>
> *Theaetetus* 210c [1]

1 *The Collected Dialogues of Plato*, ed. Edith Hamilton and Huntington Cairnes, Bollingen Series LXXI. Copyright © 1961, 1989 by Princeton University Press. Reprinted by permission of Princeton University Press.

THE *APOLOGY* OF SOCRATES

INTRODUCTION

On the surface, the *Apology* is a reconstruction of Socrates' court defense against the charges of impiety and corrupting young men brought against him by Meletos, Anytos and Lycon. Beneath this surface, however, something quite different is going on—*Philosophy is being presented as the new model of human excellence supplanting preceding models and the then current contenders aspiring towards model-status.*

We do a decided disservice to the *Apology* and to ourselves if we claim that the issue debated in this work is but the guilt or innocence, life or death of the man Socrates. The issue debated is rather the very meaning and pattern of human life itself. The issue is a life and death struggle between opposing meanings of human life, and a moral contest between opposing images of human excellence. It is a *cultural clash.*

Culture is the embodiment of the models and patterns of human excellence prevailing among a people over a period of time. Among the Hellenic peoples, such cultural models and patterns were articulated especially in poetic and religious traditions rooted in Homer. Homer was the central conduit of the Hellenic cultural tradition, and his depiction of human excellence in the *Iliad* and the *Odyssey* dominated Hellenic and Athenian life at every level. But this is to say that Poetry is the chief purveyor of the traditional model of human excellence in the Hellenic world.

In the *Apology*, Socrates will enter into a contest with Homer and, dramatically, the claim will be made that Philosophy supplants Poetry as *the* purveyor of the new model of human excellence.

The fourth century B.C. witnessed many contenders aspiring to cultural domination. Plato singled out Sophistry and Rhetoric for special consideration, although by no means did he neglect Politics and Business. Many different current contenders are presented in the *Apology* and the conclusion of the contest with Socrates is that Philosophy supplants the lot.

The *Apology*, then, is a dramatic contest between the *new morality* of Philosophy and the *old* (and current) *morality* of Poetry, Religion, Politics, Sophistry and Rhetoric. The *Apology* depicts a cultural clash and moral contest, the upshot of which is the very meaning of human life and the modelling of human excellence.

BODY

> How you felt, gentlemen of Athens, when you heard my accusers, I do not know; but I—well, I nearly forgot who I was, they were so persuasive. Yet as for truth—one might almost say they have spoken not one word of truth. 17a[1]

---

1 All translations in this and subsequent chapters, unless otherwise noted, are from *The Great Dialogues of Plato*, translated by W.H.D. Rouse, Copyright © 1956, renewed 1984 by J.C.G. Rouse. Reprinted by permission of New American Library, a division of Penguin Books, USA Inc.

The question of personal identity is underscored by these opening words. But do not presume that it is Socrates himself who is floundering. On the very contrary, for he tells us that he *nearly* forgot who he was. No, it is not Socrates' identity which is in question. It is rather the identity of the Athenians and the Hellenes and subsequently and to the extent that Plato is a major architect of Western culture, ourselves who are in question, whose identity is in danger of being "forgotten". Plato's message would seem to be that Socrates exemplifies the new model of human excellence, and to the extent that we do not understand and imitate this new model we fall short of ourselves, and we 'forget who we are'.

But cultural models, new or otherwise, do not appear out of nothing, and their emergence is contentious. Most important, perhaps, is the dynamic of discontinuity within continuity which emergence seems to impose upon successful cultural models. This dynamic has a bearing on the shape of the *Apology* and moulds its underlying structure. With respect to the continuity of cultural development, Plato will present Socrates (i.e., the philosophic pattern of behavior exemplified by Socrates) as the culmination of Hellenic excellence. With respect to the discontinuity, he will emphasize the novelty of Socrates as that which supplants tradition, the whole of tradition, and defeats upstart contenders then vying for model-status.

The *Apology* is divided into six acts: one, the proem or introduction in which Socrates separates himself from "clever speakers", and lists the two sets of accusers with whom he must contend; two, his *Odyssey* - defense[1] in which Socrates contends with his old poetic accusers, and undertakes his own "wanderings" (Odysseus like) and "labors" (Heracles like) to understand and defend

---

1 Cf. Thomas G. West, *Plato's Apology of Socrates, and interpretation with a new translations* (Ithaca and London: Cornell University Press, 1979).

the god's pronouncement concerning him; three, his *Iliad* defense in which he contends with his new poetic accusers and defeats Meletos, their spokesman; four, likening himself to Achilles and Theseus, Socrates offers himself as god's gift to Athens, and begins the delineation of Philosophy as the new model of human excellence; five, the interlude speech in which Socrates offers an alternative penalty to the death penalty demanded by his accusers, and thereby completes the supplanting of Religion by Philosophy, and six, the final remarks in which Socrates contends that philosophical examination—carried on forever in a delightful depiction of the after-life—supplants the whole of preceding Hellenic culture, and that the Philosophical hero supplants the heroes and demigods of Poetry.

To demonstrate: Act One

Socrates initiates the contest with his remarks about personal identity, and then characterizes himself as a speaker of truth and justice in opposition to the deceitful babblings of his accusers. The good guy differentiates himself immediately from the bad guys.

But not just from Meletos and company. For this is Socrates' first appearance in a court of law, and he comes before the present assembly "quite strange to the style of this place" (17d), accustomed as he is to 'plain speech' rather than to the ornamental eloquence which prevails among the Athenian judiciary. The 'plain and simple speech' of Socrates bespeaks truth and justice, and is quite foreign and opposed to the deceitfulness of rhetorical embellishments and eloquence such as prevails in the Athenian courts of law.

The contest is the more difficult for Socrates because he must contend with two sets of accusers: the old, long-standing accusers who have prejudiced the minds of Athenians for some years against him, and against whom he must contend as against shadows (shades of the lower reaches of the Cave, no less!) for none can be called forth for cross-examination, and, secondly, the contemporary, current accusers.

> The most unreasonable thing is that it is impossible to know their names or to tell who they are—unless one of them happens to be a comic poet. 18c

Poetry is singled out as *the* accuser of Socrates in these remarks, with Aristophanes representing traditional poetry. And Meletos, representing contemporary poetry, will shortly be singled out as the chief current accuser. That is to say, and already in the opening act, the contestants are clearly delineated, and the ensuing struggle will be between Philosophy and Poetry.

Each set of accusers focuses his opposition to Socrates on the latter's alleged *atheism*, the old accusers grounding the charge in its necessary connection with Natural Philosophy (with which Aristophanes clothes Socrates in the *Clouds*), and the contemporary accusers grounding the charge, quite illogically, in nothing other than a vehemently proclaimed affirmation. But more of this in act three.

Socrates concludes the proem by repeating his statement that of the two sets of accusers, the old are the much more deadly, because over the years they have instilled a deeper prejudice in the minds of the "gentlemen of Athens". Nevertheless, in obedience to "god's will" he will make his defense and try to root out this long-standing prejudice against him.

Act Two

Socrates commences act two, his *Odyssey*-quest, by reconstructing Aristophanes' old accusation "which Meletos believed when he brought this indictment" (19b), the caricaturing of Socrates as natural philosopher, sophist and teacher which the poet presented on the Athenian stage in his play, the *Clouds*. He flatly denies all three caricatures, and attributes such "stock charges" to 'bad faith' on the part of know-it-alls who would accuse anyone rather than themselves of being pretenders-to-knowledge. Furthermore, he challenges the pretentiousness of the claim-to-knowledge itself of the Natural Philosophers and the Sophists.

To the Poets as the opponents of Socrates in the *Apology*, then, we must now add the Physicists or Natural Philosophers and the Sophists.

> Some one of you then might put in and ask perhaps, "Well, Socrates, what is your business? Where did these calumnies come from?" 20c

This would indeed be a fair question, Socrates allows, and were it put to him, he would respond that a sort of wisdom has got him his name, for indeed he is wise with "perhaps the only wisdom that man can have" (20d). None other than the god of wisdom, Apollo himself, has so pronounced.

The story of Chairephon is too familiar to bear repeating. But not so Socrates' 'pious' response to the divine pronouncement. For Socrates proceeds by *disbelieving* the god, and then goes out and in exchanges with self-proclaimed wise men *he tries to prove the god wrong*! He fails in this endeavor, but not without angering the statesmen, the poets and the craftsmen.

Does he anger the god of reason, however? Does he anger Apollo?

His "testing" of the god's pronouncement that "no one was wiser" than Socrates (21a), Socrates calls his "wanderings" and "labors" (22a), i.e., his wandering and laboring to understand, to "come home to" the god's message. Plato, in other words, is saying here that Socrates is the new Odysseus and the new Heracles, the new demigod and hero of human excellence.

And piety? Socrates' piety is manifestly discontinuous with traditional religious piety. Rather than being a form of doctrinal submission or the simple repetition of traditional proclamations, Socrates' piety might perhaps be called *philosophical piety,* and it entails reservation, questioning, testing and submission only to that evidence which withstands the onslaught. And this Socratic piety, remember, is sanctioned by Apollo.

The heart of the god's message, the promulgation and defense of which constitutes Socrates' service to the god and to Athens, is the reality of human not-knowning:

> the truth really is, gentlemen, that the god in fact is wise, and in the oracle he means that human wisdom is worth little or nothing, and it appears he does not say this of Socrates, but simply adds my name to take me as an example, as if he were to say that this one of you is wisest, who like Socrates knows that he is in truth worth nothing as regards wisdom. 23 a-b

But old heroes die hard, and current contenders to cultural supremacy struggle to protect and promote themselves. Meletos has taken up the case for the poets, Anytos for the craftsmen and statesmen, and Lycon for the orators (23e).

To the Poets, the Natural Philosophers and the Sophists as the opponents of Socrates in the *Apology*, then, we must add the Craftsmen (but only to the extent that they overreach themselves and transgress their acknowledged competence), the Statesmen and the Orators.

Cultural discontinuity characterizes this second act, glazed over only with the proffered continuity of Socrates as the *new* Odysseus, the *new* Heracles and the *new* servant of Apollo.

ACT THREE

Discontinuity again prevails in the third act, in Socrates' new *Iliadic*-contest with contemporary poetry in the person of Meletos.

Socrates reads the affidavit of the contemporary accusers:

> Socrates is a criminal, who corrupts the young and does not believe in the gods whom the state believes in, but in other new spiritual things instead. 24b

In the ensuing discussion with Meletos, Socrates proceeds to demonstrate that Meletos knows nothing at all about the charges he has directed at Socrates and, moreover, that he cares nothing about any of it—all the while, of course, claiming that he (Meletos) does know and does care. *A-meles Meletos!* — "uncaring careful one".

Attempting to specify the "gods" in the affidavit, Socrates needles Meletos into charging that, fundamentally, Socrates believes in no gods at all, that he is an atheist. But by this 'clarification' Meletos contradicts himself, for he now claims that Socrates believes in gods *and* that Socrates does not believe in gods.

Even so, the contest is not really between Socrates and Meletos. It is between Philosophy and Poetry, and the point of the exchange between the two representatives is that Poetry knows-not and cares-not of what it speaks, all the while claiming the opposite. Poetry, the heart of traditional Athenian and Hellenic culture and religion, is in fact unclear and confused about its claims. It knows nothing about the gods or about the law, and it slides easily into contradictory claims. It is an unworthy purveyor of human excellence, and is here defeated, as such, in the *Iliadic*-contest with Socratic Philosophy.

ACT FOUR

So far we have been told little about Socrates' 'tactics,' and just why it is claimed that Philosophy prevails over Poetry. This is the subject matter of the fourth act.

Socrates begins by reminding the "gentlemen" of the jury that, if anything, it is their long-standing and poetically-grounded prejudice which will convict him. He continues,

> But perhaps someone will say: Are you not ashamed then, Socrates, at having followed such a practice that you now run a risk of a sentence of death? I would answer such a one fairly: You are wrong, my friend, if you think a man with a spark of decency in him ought to calculate life or death; the only thing he ought to consider, if he does anything, is whether he does right or wrong, whether it is what a good man does or a bad man. 28b

Immediately after this he casts himself in the role of Achilles, the demigod hero of poetry who in the *Iliad* despised danger and death in his pursuit of goodness and honor. The *new* Achilles recounts his staying-power at Poteidaia, Amphipolis and Delion, and then emphasizes the divine mandate of his current posting.

The goodness of the old Achilles is supplanted by that of the new Achilles, and the prowess and valor of military might is supplanted by the divinely-sanctioned duty to be a philosopher and "to test myself and others" (28e). The goodness of the poetic and military *ethos* gives way to the goodness of the philosopher, which alone vanquishes the fear of death (29a). Such a duty is the inexorable command laid upon human beings by god himself, which under no circumstances will Socrates flee.

The 'tactics' of the search-for-wisdom that is philosophy is sketched out in Socrates' reply to the suppositional we-will-let-you-off-this-time offer:

> Many thanks indeed for your kindness, gentlemen, but I will obey the god, rather than you, and as long as I have breath in me, and remain able to do it, I will never cease being a philosopher, and exhorting you, and showing what is in me to anyone of you I may meet, by speaking to him in my usual way: my excellent friend, you are an Athenian, a citizen of this great city, so famous for wisdom and strength, and you take every care to be as well off as possible in money, reputation and place—then are you not ashamed not to take every care and thought for understanding, for truth, and for the soul, so that it may be perfect? 29d-e

In the pursuit of philosophy, and in the cross-examining and testing of 'yes-men', Socrates is obeying god's commandment, "and I think there is no greater good for you in the city in any way than my service to God" (30a).

Money, reputation and place (in society) join Poetry as purveyors of the old morality which is to be supplanted by Socrates' new morality, by his "care and thought for understanding, for truth, and for the soul, so that it may be perfect"(29e)—by Philosophy.

Indeed, pursuit of philosophy has necessitated not only that Socrates neglect his own monetary, reputational and positional interests, but also that he separate himself from political activity:

> the fact is that no man in the world will come off safe who honestly opposes either you or any other multitude, and tries to hinder the many unjust and illegal doings in a state. It is necessary that one who really and truly fights for the right, if he is to survive even for a short time, shall act as a private man, not as a public man. 31e-32a

Politics, then, joins the bad guys.

Nor is Socrates a teacher (33a), and he cannot justly be held accountable for how any of his young friends turn out "when I never promised any learning to anyone and never taught any" (33b). Young friends have followed him a-plenty, however, for it "is not unpleasant" (32b) for them to hear the pretentiousness of their elders punctured. That the witnessing of such cross-examining has *not* corrupted any of them is attested by the fact that none of the pairs of fathers and brothers and seven young friends enumerated has arisen to charge him.

Socrates concludes the act by arguing that the very integrity of his defense—that he did not utilize the weeping and wailing of his wife and children on his behalf—is itself indicative of the falseness of the charges brought against him, and especially of the charge of atheism: "I am far from that, gentlemen; I do believe, in a sense in which none of my accusers does" (35d).

I cannot conclude my discussion of this fourth act without calling attention to Socrates' enumeration of the two groups of seven, or the seven pairs, in section 33d-34a. Only in one other place in Plato's writings are we given such an extended and precise enumeration, *Phaedo* 59 b-c, and there the enumeration of fourteen is used to cast Socrates in the role of Theseus, the Athenian hero who saved himself and the group of seven boys and seven girls from death by the Cretan Minotaur. By extension, Socrates as the new Theseus saves himself, his fourteen enumerated friends and Athens from death by Misology. Is Plato here inviting us to connect the Socrates of the *Apology* with the Theseus-Socrates of the *Phaedo*? Or rather, if as seems likely the *Phaedo* is a later composition than the *Apology*, is Plato inviting us to connect the Socrates of the *Phaedo* with the Socrates of the *Apology*? Whichever dialogue precedes which, I believe Plato is inviting us to connect the two, and just what we are to make of the connection is an interesting question.

ACT FIVE

In his speech between the two votings, Socrates assures the "gentlemen of Athens" that he is neither resentful nor surprised at their finding him guilty as charged. In fact, he is surprised at the paltry margin that his accusers realized.

But he does not let up on his defense of Philosophy for one moment, nor on his criticism and cross-examining of Athenian morality. He does this—his divinely-appointed-duty, remember—with his playful yet serious interpretation of the penalty to be imposed upon him by the court. His accusers propose death as the appropriate penalty. Now the word for "penalty" also means "worth". Socrates adopts the second meaning, as it were, and proposes that he "be boarded free in the town hall" (36d) as commensurate with his "worth" to the city.

Is this a playful juggling of the ambiguity of the Greek word? I think so, yes. But, more importantly, it is a direct assault on traditional Athenian piety and religious values. The "town hall" is the hearth or heart of the city. It was the holiest of holies, the divine-grounding of the city's laws and customs and the surety of values and oaths. Socrates, who believes "in a sense in which none of my accusers does" (35d), is usurping this center, and most dramatically proclaiming that Philosophy supplants Religion as the hearth and center of political life!

And the justification for such arrogance?

> I tried to persuade each one of you to take care of himself first, and how he could become most good and most wise, before he took care for any of his interests, and to take care for the state herself first before he took care of any of her interests: that in other things also, this was the proper order of his care.36c

The Olympian victors traditionally boarded in the "town hall" contribute only to *seeming* happiness, "but" Socrates claims, "I make you be happy" (36e).

Might I conclude from this that the gods sheltering Olympian victors were only *seemingly* divine, while the god sheltering Socrates actually *is* divine? I believe I can.

Perhaps not to appear entirely adamant in his arrogance, Socrates goes on to propose a modest fine which he can afford, and then he proposes a stiffer fine because his friends have promised to pay it. But he does this only after reiterating his conviction that he has "never willingly wronged anyone" (37a), and that his discussions of virtue and his examining himself and everybody else is "the greatest good for man" (38a), and that "life without inquiry is not worth living for a man" (38a)— more commonly, "the unexamined life is not worth living".

Needless to say, and as we well know, the court condemns Socrates to death; that is to say, the court assigns the penalty/worth of death to Socrates' behavior as a philosopher.

Act Six

The final act is composed of four short addresses, two to the "gentlemen of Athens" who voted to condemn and execute Socrates and two to the "judges" ("for you I could rightly call judges" 40a) who voted to acquit him.

In the first address directed to his condemners, Socrates berates the pseudo-judges for taking offence at his not approaching them in the customary and pleading manner. Such an approach, he insists, would have been unworthy of himself, of themselves, and of the city. He prophesies that critics will arise to accuse them and the city of having executed a wise man. He declares that they have let wickedness overtake them,

> and now I, being slow and old, have been caught by the slower one; but my accusers, being clever and quick, have been caught by the swifter, badness. 39b

To the judges he declares that what has happened is a wonderful thing, as demonstrated by the failure of his "familiar prophetic voice" (40a), "the signal of God" (40b), to stop him from coming to the court in the morning or checking him while speaking, as it has done before when he was about to say anything inappropriate or embark on any unworthy course of action.

Death, then, cannot be an evil, but would rather seem to be something good, being either an uninterrupted sleep or, "as people say, a change and a migration for the soul from this place here to another place" (40c). And were it the latter, "what greater good" (40e) could happen to a person? Here Socrates launches into his depiction of the philosopher's heaven which caps the supplanting of Poetry and Religion by Philosophy. For

> to go on cross-examining the people there, as I did those here, and investigating, which of them is wise, and which thinks he is, but is not! How much would one give, judges of the court, to cross-examine him who led the great invasion against Troy or Odysseus or Sisyphos, or thousands of other men and women? To converse with them there, and to be with them, and cross-examine them would be an infinity of happiness! 41b-c

Socrates' final words are, again, addressed to the judges, with but a segment directed to the pseudo-judges who voted to condemn and execute him. To the judges he offers encouragement that they recognize that "no evil can happen to a good man either living or dead" (41d). To the pseudo-judges he offers exculpation and a corrective to their self-inflicted wickedness:

> Punish my sons, gentlemen, when they grow up; give them the same pain I gave you, if you think they care for money or anything

> else before virtue; and if they have the reputation of being something when they are nothing, reproach them, as I reproach you, that they do not care for what they should, and think they are something when they are worth nothing. And if you do this, we shall have been justly dealt with by you, both I and my sons. 41e-42a

CONCLUSION

Let me recapitulate. Socrates is on trial, charged with impiety and corrupting the young. The penalty asked for is death. The *Apology* is Socrates' response to these charges, and yet his defense does not at all demonstrate his innocence of the charges. Rather, he loquaciously displays his breach with traditional morality, parades his heroic and demigodly uniqueness, and arrogantly challenges the Athenians to transcend their tradition and follow him into what could only have been considered by that tradition itself an impious and corrupting venture.

Guilty as charged? Absolutely!

Nor, having been pronounced guilty by the court, does he let up his pestering one bit. Convinced that he never wronged anyone, and further convinced that his inquiries and goadings contribute to making people actually happy rather than seemingly happy, Socrates demands as his penalty/worth free board in the town hall. A proposal of exile most likely would have been accepted by the court. Not only will he not make such a proposal, but he states that even his consideration of the penalty of exile would be unreasonable and motivated by a 'foolish fondness of life'. And to consider "keeping silent" would be to fly in the face of god's commandment.

In many and persistent ways, Socrates challenges the "gentlemen of Athens". His arrogance and posturing is best understood, I think, in the context of the cultural confrontation between the old and the new moralities and images of human excellence, and in the religious context of divine mission and salvational message.

The contest acted out in the *Apology* is not to be taken lightly. It does not, at least directly, concern the life and death of the man Socrates. What is at issue, rather, is the salvation of the human soul, the salvation of humanity. What is at issue is the deliverance of humanity, through the person and behavior of Socrates, from its forgetfulness of its own identity and authentically human possibilities. A new image of human excellence, a veritable transformation of the traditional image, is offered us in the philosophy of Socrates, and we ignore it at our own peril.

Even as Homer was the acknowledged teacher of Hellas, and even as Homer taught primarily by modelling human excellence in heroes and demigods, so Plato becomes the *new* teacher (of Hellas and of her descendants), and he teaches by modelling the new and transformed image of human excellence in the person and behavior of Socrates.

Cultural and modelling continuity pervades this pedagogical project, and so Plato will cast Socrates in decidedly Homeric and heroic roles. Successively, he will liken Socrates to Odysseus and Heracles in his wanderings and labors, to Achilles in refusing to calculate death before disgrace, and to Theseus in his embarking with the group of fourteen on the not-unpleasant voyage of cross-examining those who think they are wise but are not. Finally, in his depiction of the philosopher's heaven, Plato casts Socrates in the role almost of a god passing judgement on the many demigods and heroes the Hellenes paraded before themselves as models of human excellence. Socrates supplants the lot!

Socrates' (Apollonian) piety receives a great deal of attention in this trial circumscribed by the religious festival honoring Apollo.

Indeed, Socrates is Apollo's gift to Athens, a gadfly sent to quicken the lumbering thoroughbred that is the State. Socrates is the messenger from god bearing the new words of quickening, the new words of righteousness and of salvation.

In the act of traditional-embodiments-and-reincarnations, Socrates contradicts tradition and turns it upside down (Cf. *Gorgias* 381 b-c). So also, charged with impiety and corrupting the young, Socrates turns the tables on Athens and the Hellenic tradition and, before himself as the embodiment of the new *arete*, pronounces *them* guilty! Socrates, then, is *not* guilty as charged.

The new Homeric hero fights not for booty and military honor, but for truth and justice and for the "soul" that it might be as perfect as possible. The new hero does not fear and bemoan his death, but insists on one's duty not to fear the unknown, and humorously (but seriously, supplanting poetic religion) paints a picture of the philosophical afterlife as entailing an infinity of happiness of endless cross-examination.

Perhaps the transformation of tradition is focused most sharply in Socrates' transformation of piety. Indeed, Socrates does believe in a sense in which none of his accusers or contemporaries does. His initial response to Apollo's revelation that none was wiser than he was outright incredulity, followed immediately by his labors to contest the god and prove him a liar! The *new* piety entails reservation, criticism and submission only to that evidence which withstands the testing and cross-examination, all the while remaining fully conscious of the heart of the revelation which has withstood the assault, "that human wisdom is worth little or nothing."

And *this* is the new image and model of human excellence offered to us in the person and behavior of Socrates. *This* is Philosophy.

And so the curtain falls on the last act, and the audience and readers are left to assimilate the message proffered as best they can. Nor is there anything concrete or definitive about the message of the *Apology*.

Rather, we are left with a number of essential questions: how does one "take every care and thought for understanding, for truth, and for the soul, so that it may be perfect?" (29d-e) What is this "soul"? and what is "truth" and "understanding" in light of the not-knowing that is so emphasized in this dialogue? Finally, how does one "think" and *do* philosophy?

The *Apology* prepares the ground, but it is the related dialogues alluded-to in it which will delineate the method of *thinking* and *doing philosophy* which will bear fruit only in the quickening of our own lives.

THE *MENO*, OR ENQUIRY CHECKED

I can imagine no more improbable a dialogue than one taking place between the stodginess of a Menon ("stay-put") and the inquisitiveness of a Socrates. And yet Plato presents just such a dialogue as occurring in his work, the *Meno*.

The very improbability of such ever taking place (realistically *or* dramatically) has not, I think been appreciated sufficiently in our own philosophic tradition, a tradition which we ourselves, generally speaking, see solidly rooted in Plato.

What, then, is going on in the *Meno*? How far does the dialogue progress, and, indeed, is it a dialogue at all?

Approaching these in the reverse order of presentation, let me say immediately, yes, of course it is a dialogue. There is a great deal of dia-loguing, talking-together, going on in there. And progress? Of course; a great deal of progress is made—but only on the part of two characters in the play, I think, the slave-boy and Socrates. Menon at one point *seems* to have progressed, at least to the point of appearing to recognize his own ignorance—no small an achievement in itself if it really happens, any friend of Socrates will admit. But this is only seeming, for as soon as he catches his breath he is right back "bullying"

Socrates from his original position ("stay-put"). And Anytos? Anytos not only does not progress during the dialogue itself, but he already here presents us with a clear statement of the very attitude and position he will adopt some three (dramatic) years hence in the trial of Socrates.

Progress is made by the slave-boy. He moves from a state of ignorance regarding the solution of the geometrical problem presented to him to the discovery of the solution. I shall return to this.

And progress is made by Socrates. Yes indeed. But it is not immediately apparent just what this progress is, and exactly how this progress is made, because that progress can only be measured in the actual progress made by the audience/readers.

So I'm back with my first question. What is going on in the *Meno*? What do *we* understand of what is going on there, and how has our understanding progressed from the beginning to the end of the dialogue?

What is going on, then, is very little on the surface, and has been outlined by R.S. Bluck in his edition of the *Meno* as covering five stages:

1. the question, "can virtue be taught?" (70a), is quickly reduced to the question, What is virtue itself? The interlocutors fail to define virtue, and Menon is reduced to numbness;

2. Menon challenges Socrates: "And how will you try to find out something, Socrates, when you have no notion at all what it is?" (80d)—to which Socrates responds with his declaration that the human soul is immortal and that knowledge is recollection, and proceeds to illustrate the same in discussion with the slave-boy;

3. Menon again asks whether virtue can be taught, and Socrates agrees to pursue the question using the hypothetical method envisaged by the geometricians. He concludes that virtue would appear to be knowledge and to be teachable;

4. further analysis reveals the teachability of virtue to be highly suspect, for there are no generally-accepted teachers of this supposed knowledge. Perhaps virtue is not knowledge or teachable after all;

5. he concludes that "virtue is seen as coming neither by nature nor by teaching" (99e), unless some politician can be found so outstanding as to make others politicians after the fashion of himself.[1]

The usual interpretation of this runs something as follows: the first part of the dialogue leading up to the numbing of Menon is a typical early Socratic dialogue. Ostensibly, a definition is being sought either of virtue or of virtue's "teachableness," and Socrates, with his usual ironic midwifery, demolishes the pretentiousness of his interlocutor and the two of them end up knowing that they know nothing;

But the *Meno* does not stay-put with this early elenctic posturing. The tone of the discussion is raised to a higher pitch, and Socrates embarks on a meta-elenctic, positive interpretation of knowing;

In response to Menon's inquiry into the very possibility of knowing/searching itself, Socrates affirms that the human soul is

---

1 Cf. J.E. Raven, *Plato's Thought in the Making* (Cambridge: Cambridge University Press, 1965), p.58.

really immortal, and knowing/searching in this life is grounded in recollection of the ideas and realities known in our previous life;

As a concrete demonstration of the above, Socrates elicits from the slave-boy a knowing of geometrical deciphering that clearly manifests apriority/innatism;

The discussion now returns to the original question. Is virtue teachable? And Socrates and Menon using the hypothetical method of mathematics/geometry conclude that it seems likely that virtue is not teachable;

Opinion is distinguished from knowledge. The operative virtue in Hellas is recognized as being opinion, and the conclusion is drawn that virtue is teachable, but only under the guidance of 'Socrates' himself:

> But if we have ordered all our enquiry well and argued well, virtue is seen as coming neither by nature nor by teaching; but by divine allotment incomprehensibly to those to whom it comes-unless there were some politician so outstanding as to be able to make another man a politician. (99e-100a)

And all of this is understood quite *literally*, and the gist of the *Meno* is seen to lie in the grounding of epistemic recollection in the realistic pre-viewing of Ideas!

Of course I consider this traditional interpretation somewhat of a bumbling fantasy, and I offer instead an interpretation of the *Meno* as an *explication of the logic of hypothetical reasoning*, itself being a concrete demonstration of this actual (and proper) method of reasoning/thinking.

Such an interpretation *(i.e. hypothesis)* has the immediate effect of tying the whole dialogue together, and sets up the possibility of tying together the so-called "middle" and "later" dialogues in a manner quite beyond the capabilities of the traditional interpretation. If coherence, then, has any "truth-value" associated with it, such a *hypothetical-methodological* interpretation would seem, initially, to be much "truer" than the traditional metaphysical-epistemological interpretation.

But coherence is no more an infallible indication of truth-value than is traditional acceptance. Perhaps one of the lessons we can learn from Plato is that there is no such thing as infallible indication at all.

Let me see, then, if I can 'tie-down' my hypothesis to the text of the *Meno*.

The opening scene of the *Meno,* when interpreted methodologically, is seen to be not so much another elenctic discussion, as it becomes a concrete demonstration by Socrates of definitional and deductive logic. Socrates very carefully and systematically lays it out before Menon who is too puffed up with his own 'learning' to see it. But do we see it ourselves?

Menon initiates the discussion by asking Socrates:

> can virtue be taught? Or if not, does it come by practice? Or does it come neither by practice nor by teaching, but do people get it by nature, or in some other way? 70a

Socrates very patiently responds that we can hardly begin to pursue such questions until we have come to some prior agreement as to what virtue itself is. And in the ensuing exchanges he maintains: (a) that the definition (that should be) sought must be an *essential* definition, a statement of what constitutes virtue as such, and is, accordingly, identical in the many instances ("swarm") of virtue; and, (b) that the constituents of this definition are to be simple, independently known and agreed to—which later came to be referred to as "Occam's razor", and when absent and as a consequent fallacy, *petio principi.*

What on the surface appears as simple elenctic discussion presents itself deeper down as the systematic elaboration of a satisfactory method of forming definitions, as what I have already called an exercise in *definitional logic*. And the very method of pursing definitions that Socrates recommends in this opening scene will be seen later on to be understood more properly as a hypothesis. Definitional logic, then, becomes (or at least becomes contained within) *hypothetical logic*.

Menon, of course, scarcely appreciates the formal clarifications being demonstrated, and, predictably, accuses Socrates of sorcery and of drowning him in puzzledom:

> Well now, my dear Socrates, you are just like what I always heard before I met you:always puzzled yourself and puzzling every-body else ... your looks and the rest of you are exactly like a flatfish and you sting like this stingray — only go near and touch one of those fish and you go numb, and that is the sort of thing you seem to have done to me. 79e - 80a[1]

Socrates replies that the metaphor is appropriate only if the fish itself is numb as well as numbing, for indeed he is now just as numb and just as ignorant as Menon on the question of what virtue is. More importantly, however, he draws a clear distinction between the numbness of Menon which *binds* him in ignorance and his own numbness which *opens* him to the pursuit of what he now knows he lacks. (The slave-boy shortly will imitate Socrates' numbness rather then Menon's.)

---

1 But he further goes on to say that the metaphor of *touching* is quite inaccurate, else Socrates, who had been touched by Menon, would now be as filled with knowledge as Menon so thought himself when he touched Socrates.

Menon rejoins with his famous argument, "chop-logic" Socrates calls it, that it is impossible to search out anything, either what we do not now know, for how would we look for what we would not know even if we found it; nor for what we now know, for what, then, would we search out?

Socrates reacts quite appropriately to this denial of the very possibility of questioning, examining, pursuing *by showing the same in operation* in the very activity of the slave-boy discovering the solution to the geometrical problem presented to him.

But we are not quite ready for this scene yet. Socrates introduces first the important theme of recollection. It is absolutely important that we appreciate what is going on here. He considers Menon's objection a piece of "chop-logic", contentiousness, and replies that he objects to the objection because he has "heard wise men and women on the subject of things divine":

> The speakers were some priests and priestesses who have paid attention to the things of their ministry, so as to be able to give a reasoned explanation of them; also inspired poets have something to say... .81a - 81b —

a story to the effect that the human soul is immortal, is subject to innumerable reincarnations in the course of which it has seen everything "in Hades and on earth," and therefore learning here is nothing other then remembering or recollecting what it saw there.

There is at least one interesting internal analysis of this tale that can be carried out—the seeming infinite regress involved in remembering/learning/remembering, *etc.* But far more important, I think, is the external analysis focusing on the character of the priests and priestesses (the bearers of the message) in question: Socrates explicitly characterizes these people as having paid careful attention to their ministry "*so as to be able to give a reasoned explanation* ..." (Italics added). His characterization of the poets in question as "inspired" has the same effect, and which effect will not become clarified until almost the very end of the dialogue. Let us now simply keep in mind, then, that this story *is* qualified, and is qualified in a manner that seems peculiarly methodological.

But under no circumstances are we to ignore the singular character with which Socrates distinguishes his own attitude from that of Menon: *Socrates' way makes people active and enquiring,* whereas Menon's makes people idle "and it is pleasant for soft people to hear" (81d). Socrates now calls in Menon's slave-boy to demonstrate just this point, to demonstrate the very possibility of active inquisitiveness leading to successful completion *by showing it in action.*[1]

I am aware that I am here deviating from the traditional interpretation of this scene. My own attitude is complex: on the one hand, it seems to me that there is no overly strong textual basis to support one over the other, and, on the other hand, my interpretation takes into account various nuances and statements in the text that the other does not. But the central support for my thesis, I think, comes from the scene which immediately follows this geometrical demonstration, and which formally articulates the methodological procedure which the geometrical exercise concretizes step by step. Let me see if I can document this.

Socrates' concluding remarks of the analysis of the geometrical demonstration are as follows:

---

1 I am in debt to John Sallis' insistence on *ergon* in this scene, although my overall treatment of the same differs somewhat, I think, from his. Cf. John Sallis, *Being and Logos, The Way of Platonic Dialogue* (Pittsburgh: Duquesne University Press, 1975).

> Yes, I would think that I argue well, Menon,I would not be confident in everything I say about the argument; but one thing I would fight for to the end, both in word and in deed if I were able — that *if we believed that we must try to find out what is not known*, we should be better and braver and less idle than if we believed that what we do not know it is impossible to find out and that we need not even try. 86b-c (Italics added)

Menon immediately bullies Socrates into discussing the teachableness of virtue without first enquiring into virtue itself. Socrates submits to the pressure. That is to say, *Socrates agrees to enquire into what is not known*, and specifies that, such being the case, *we must proceed by way of hypothesis*. Let me quote the relevant passage in full.

> But if I were your master, Menon, as well as master of myself, we should not consider beforehand whether virtue can be taught or not until we had tried to find out first what virtue really is. But since you make no attempt to master yourself — I suppose you want to be a free man — but you do attempt to master me, and you do master me! I will give way to you—for what else am I to do?—and it seems we must consider what qualities a thing has when we don't know yet what it is. Please relax at least one little title of your mastery, and give way so far that we may use a hypothesis to work from, in considering whether it can come by teaching or in some other way, I mean by hypothesis what the geometricians often envisage, a standing ground to start from ...
>
> There now, let us take virtue in that way. Since we don't know what it is or what it is like, let us make our hypothesis or ground to stand on, and then consider whether it can be taught or not. 86d-87b

And what follows this in a protracted exchange between Socrates and Menon is a *concrete exemplification of the hypothetical /scientific method!* [1] Very carefully and methodically Socrates proceeds through the various stages of laying down hypotheses, clarifying and explicating the hypotheses, deducing various consequences from these hypotheses, and lastly, *empirically* testing the same.[2]

Now let me go back to the slave-boy scene. Two points immediately jump to our attention. One, the whole demonstration presents itself as a concrete exemplification of this hypothetical method. Two, the hypothetical method is predicated ultimately upon immediate perception. For example, Socrates calls the slave-boy over to ask him to draw a square double the size of any given square. He begins by drawing a picture of a square, presenting it to the boy saying, this is a square, do you understand (see it)? The boy replies, yes. Now had he not replied yes, had he not 'immediately' perceived meaning on this minimal point, the resulting demonstration never would have gotten off the ground. The boy sees; Socrates can neither see for him nor make him see! And *this* is the significant point Socrates makes with his repeated assertion that he *teaches* the boy nothing, that the boy *learns nothing from Socrates.*

From this initial understanding Socrates carefully presents the question to the boy, and the boy very shortly answers, i.e., *lays down the hypothesis,* that a square double the size of any given square must

---

1 Cf. Alexandre Koyré, *Discovering Plato* (New York: Columbia University Press, 1945), p.15, n.12.

2 This point is of crucial importance, although I would not want to put undue emphasis on the word "empirical". "Experiential" is perhaps better. But the point is that Plato digs around to see whether or not the predicted consequences work, are present in experience.

have any one side double the length of any one side of the given square. The hypothesis is then clarified, diagrammed and tested, and the boy '*immediately*' perceives that the hypothesis results in a square four-times the given square rather than the predicted two-times. He admits that he was wrong, that his hypothesis is discredited/falsified. And so on, until he works out what we call the Pythagorean Theorem, the square on the hypotenuse is the sum of the squares on the other two sides.

Recollection of pre-existentially-viewed mathematicals? Hardly. Hypothetical empiricism!

But there is another point that has been glossed over that is of crucial importance, I think, and will now dominate the remainder of the dialogue:

> Since we don't know what it is or what it is like, let us make our hypothesis or ground to stand on, and then consider whether it can be taught or not. 87b

The remaining dialogue posits, clarifies, deduces and tests varying hypotheses concerning the teachableness of virtue, and concludes that virtue is probably not teachable because no empirical instances of the same can be found.

But that is not what is really central here, I think. Look at the statement again: when we don't know what something is or is like, we proceed with our investigation of the same by means of the hypothetical method. Fine. But can we turn this around? Can we interpret Socrates as here saying that *whenever we use the hypothetical method we do so precisely to the extent that we do not know the object of our search, either what it is or what it is like?*

I believe we can, while believing at the same time that I will not be able to document this definitively in the dialogues. Definitive documentation: Plato provides us with many instances of definite *negative* documentation/demonstration. He quite clearly operates according to the model that negative verification, falsification, destroys/dis-proves the hypothesis. He never offers us instances of confirmation positively verifying hypotheses as true. However, he does offer us many instances of agreement/confirmation indicating the *likely* character of hypotheses. Was Plato aware, then, that positive confirmation/verification merely demonstrates the *not-incorrectness* of hypotheses, but never their correctness? I believe he was.

But let us return to the *Meno* and to the two interesting points remaining, and which might help to shed some light on my hypothesizing in this essay.

Anytos, who replaces Menon for one scene discussing whether or not virtue can be taught, reacts violently to the suggestion that the Sophists might properly be considered teachers of virtue. He loudly exclaims that he has never had anything at all to do with Sophists, and yet knows "whether I have experiences of them or not": that they are a "manifest canker and destruction" (91c) to men and cities.

Socrates replies:

> Astonishing! Then how could you know anything about this matter, whether there is anything good or bad in it, if you are quite without experience of it?

and he concludes:

> Perhaps you are a prophet, Anytos; since how indeed otherwise you could know about them, from what you say yourself, I should wonder. 92c

What is the role of Anytos in the dialogue? The traditional interpretation places him there more or less as a representative of the thoughtless and prejudiced Athenian conservatives who would eventually do Socrates in. Yes, I'll buy that. I think this is part of the picture. But much more important, I think, is the posturing Plato gives to Anytos, and which posturing quite clearly demonstrates wherein Anytos' thoughtlessness and prejudice lie. They lie in his refusal to recognize his own hypothetical reasoning, and in the vehemence with which he attacks Socrates' "disrespectful" questioning rather than question his own beliefs and statements.

But he also plays an ironic-type role, an almost Socratic-type role, casting doubt back on the earlier discussion of recollection. I think this dimension (quite conscious of the part of Plato, and unconscious on the part of Anytos) of Anytos' role serves to underscore the hypothetical character of the original recollection-statements, and a hypothetical character, by the way, that was not methodically worked-out, was not properly delineated. I think Plato is here saying, look, be careful, recollection is not what it seems to be, and the whole question has to be worked out much more carefully and systematically than was ever attempted there.

Anytos departs and Socrates and Menon continue the discussion into virtue's teachability, concentrating now on the *de facto* lack of actual teachers and the abounding confusion among the Sophists and poets regarding the same. The conclusions of this hypothetical arguing, quite unmistakably, is that probably virtue cannot be taught. Menon extends this conclusion and asks "whether there are good men at all, or what could be the way in which the good men who exist come into being" (96d)?

Quite apart from the fact that Menon is still seeking the qualities or consequences of an unknown (and in a supposedly non-hypothetical manner) before seeking out that unknown—Menon does, indeed, stay-put—this serves to introduce the last and very interesting point to be discussed in the dialogue, the distinction we are to draw between true opinion and knowledge.

But before we pursue this matter, I think we ought attend very carefully to what has been accomplished so far, and, specifically, to the motion or lack-of-motion of old Stay-put in this particular scene.

Menon here, then, once again raises the question of whether or not virtue/goodness can be taught/transmitted without first enquiring into the nature of the virtue or goodness in question. Socrates had balked originally at pursuing this type of questioning. He does not now. Rather he raises the possibility—recognizing now the entire *legitimacy* of Menon's line of questioning—that perhaps they had better double-check their own reasoning; perhaps, *given the utter impracticability of their conclusion*, they have overlooked something in their own reasoning.

But let us look a little more closely at the now current legitimacy of Menon's "staying-put".

Between these two requests of Menon's, of course, lies the formulation of the hypothetical method, and Socrates' insistence that when pursuing an unknown we necessarily proceed hypothetically. The legitimacy of Menon's second request is grounded in hypothesizing as so outlined by Socrates. His first request—formally identical with the second—was not then legitimate because the hypothetical method had not then been specified/developed.

Socrates clearly perceives the distinction involved. Does Menon? And, more importantly, do we?

Regardless, Socrates responds to Menon's objection and introduces the distinction between knowledge and true/right opinion:

> And so long as he has a right opinion about that of which the other has knowledge, he will be quite as good a guide as the one who knows, although he does not know, but only thinks, what is true. 97b

and again,

> Then true opinion is no worse than wisdom, for rightness of action; and this is what we failed to see just now while we were enquiring what sort of a thing virtue is. We said then that wisdom alone guides to right action; but, really, true opinion does the same. 97b

And now Socrates introduces his famous simile of Daidalos. Right/true opinions, *as opinions*, are like the statues of Daidalos; they climb down off their pedestals and run away. Knowledge, on the other hand, is a fastening-down of such right and true opinions:

> If left loose there is not much value in owning one of his works — like a runaway slave; it doesn't stay; but chained up it is worth a great deal; for they are fine works of art. What am I driving at? Why, at true opinions. For the true opinions, as long as they stay, are splendid and do all the good in the world; but they will not stay long-off and away they run out of the soul of mankind, so they are not worth much until you fasten them up with the reasoning of cause and effect. But this, my dear Menon, is remembering, as we agreed before. When they are fastened up, first they become knowledge, secondly they remain; and that is why knowledge is valued more than right opinion, and differs from right opinion by this bond. 97e-98a

"Reasoning and cause and effect ... remembering" is *hypothetical reasoning*, the clarification and working-out of which we have been pursuing, is what the *Meno* is all about.[1]

But complexity builds upon complexity. Notice what Socrates says next:

> Well, I speak by conjecture, not as one who knows; but to say that right opinion is different from knowledge, that, I believe, is no conjecture in me at all. That I would say I know; there are few things I would say that of, but this I would certainly put down as one of those I know. 98b

What is happening here? Conjecture is hypothesis, and Socrates seems to be saying that he *un-hypothetically* posits knowledge as distinct from opinions, and, hypothetically, that the one (knowledge) is distinct from the other (opinion) by this very method of hypothesizing.

---

1 Cf. Raoul Naroll, "The Logic of Generalization," in *A Handbook of Method in Cultural Anthropology*, ed. by Raoul Naroll and Ronald Cohen (New York and London: Columbia University Press, 1973), P. 25:

"I put it to you that there is no way to answer with certainty. There is no way to be absolutely sure. There is no final and clear answer to the question of the Chinese paradox: 'How do you know that you are not now dreaming?' ... Ever since the basic issues were raised by Plato and Aristotle, thoughtful men in the West have wondered and disagreed about the basic nature of knowledge."

In a thoughtfully probing investigation of the logic of knowing, Naroll delineates what he calls "stochastic epistemology," *i.e.* a theory of knowing as a process of deductive theorizing and drawing probability inferences in terms of structured empirical attempts at verification (*i.e.* refutation).

Of course Naroll sees deductive reasoning being first formally clarified/worked-out by Popper. I see it as already having been tackled by Plato!

Absolute certitude? Far from it, indeed! Rather does it seem to be a 'definitive' statement of the methodological difference between knowledge and opinion, without at the same time claiming absolute status for either. Knowledge, it says, is that which we posit (at least in this instance), talk about and defend. It is never what we absolutely know.

Nor is talking and defending to be identified with *teaching*. Socrates quite consistently separated himself from the teachers of virtue, and here towards the end of the dialogue he designates politicians, oracle-chanters, diviners, and poets as practitioners of right opinion, knowing "nothing of what they say" (99c). Right opinion can be *taught* no more than can knowledge, and the improvement of our human lot, then, would seem to fall between "divine allotment incomprehensibly" and "some politician so outstanding as to be able to make another man a politician"(100a).

But this is a most confusing (numbing) conclusion to the dialogue! On the one hand, the "outstanding politicians" I interpret as a reference to Socrates himself, and, on the other hand, it tells us nothing; it leaves us numb. Whether this is the numbness of a Menon or of a Socrates is perhaps left to each of us to decide for ourselves.

But is the enquiry checked, as the title of the dialogue might seem to indicate? *Virtue* cannot be taught. *Knowledge* cannot be taught. The one, supposedly, comes to us by divine dispensation; the other, by recollection. Enquiry, indeed, would seem to be check-mated, as I believe it is for Menon and Anytos:

> unless there were some politician so outstanding as to be able to make another man a politician. And if there were one, he might almost be said to be among the living such as Homer says of Teiresias among the dead, for Homer says of him that he alone of those in Hades has his mind, the others are flittering shades. In the same way also here on earth

> such a man would be, in respect of virtue, as something real amongst shadows. (100a)

No, indeed, Socrates cannot *teach* virtue, but nonetheless he is the most virtuous, the most real of human beings. He will make no-one a politician, although he is himself politically eminent. Socrates does not *teach,* but he does himself *demonstrate* and *image* mind and reality. It is only through our imitating this Socratic imitation, this Socratic *methodos,* that we ourselves shall attain mind and reality.

CONCLUDING REMARKS

The deeper I think I'm getting into the *Meno* the more complexities I perceive. For instance, Socrates seems to posit a formal/methodological distinction between his own thinking and the thinking of priests, politicians and poets, *but not a substantial/true distinction* - "right opinion is nothing inferior to knowledge, and will be no less useful for actions..."(98c). The myth of recollection, then, can indeed be understood literally. My metaphorical interpretation is unnecessary, and the traditional one is quite adequate. Plato, then, did posit recollection and pre-existence-viewing of intelligibles, even though he did not "tie it down" quite securely!

But let us not be too hasty.

Socrates surrounds his reiteration of that myth with qualifying statements that have not been sufficiently attended to. He concludes that scene, you remember:

> Then we must not be guided by this chop-logic argument; for this would make us idle, and it is pleasant for soft people to hear, but our way makes them active and enquiring. I have faith that this is true. . . 81-e

"I have faith that this is true," *i.e.*, I have faith that active enquiry will bear fruit, that people can learn and, indeed, do learn. And, of course, the immediately following discussion with the slave-boy demonstrates just this. That is to say, it demonstrates that people can and do learn through hypothetical enquiry. It does *not* demonstrate recollective pre-existence.

And the introductory qualifier is, if anything, even more interesting:

> The speakers were some priests and priestesses who have paid careful attention to the things of their ministry, so as to be able to give a reasoned explanation of them ... .81a

Of course, the ensuing myth is *anything but* a *reasoned explanation*, no more than is the Gorgias-type definition of color a better definition than the Socrates-type definition of figure. The point at issue is that the purported "reasoned explanation" is no *reasoned explanation* at all!

Indeed, even the purported "all nature is akin" dimension (81d) of recollection points rather to the *possibility* of a "reasoned explanation" than to the facts that such has here been offered.

> For since all nature is akin, and the soul has learnt everything, there is nothing to hinder a man, remembering one thing only—which men call learning—from himself finding out all else, if he is brave and does not weary in seeking; for seeking and learning is all remembrance. 81d

That is to say, 'remembering' how to learn, or learning the proper method of learning itself, we can then pursue knowledge and discover reasoned explanations even as the slave-boy shortly demonstrates.

Does Plato, then, posit pre-existence? And does he, quite literally, ground knowing in remembering/recollecting 'previewed' intelligibles? I suggest that there is no indication whatsoever for this in the dialogue.

What, then, is the *Meno* all about?

I suggest that the *Meno* is a concentrated and dramatically concrete working-out of the logic of hypothetical reasoning; that such reasoning is here offered as the only method available to us, to "tie-down", to delineate and defend affirmations and commitments; that such reasoning, while being the best use of the means and resources available to us, is nevertheless and inevitably *problematic* and *hypothetical*.

But we can know. Of course. And we can, indeed, touch the absolute. Yes of course. Could anyone—could Plato—admiring Socrates ever think otherwise? But if we are to be human beings; if we are to become better human beings, we must examine, pursue and energetically enquire so as to touch more, and to touch more consistently and reliably.

Where, then, does this leave us with right opining and knowing? On the one hand it leaves us exactly where Plato leaves us: materially, and for practical purposes (and knowledge for Plato is related inevitably to practical purposes), there is no distinction whatsoever between the two. Formally, however, there can be a great deal of difference between them, for just when I might want to use the one, right opinion, it might have escaped me, and therefore the necessity to convert it into the other, knowledge.

And Plato is quite clear in this dialogue that when dealing with unknown variables the proper method of knowing, the *only* method of knowing available to us, is the *hypothetical* method. The *Meno,* as

I've already stated, would seem to be a working-out of the logic of such hypothetical knowing.

Now I cannot adequately document this, and I'm going way beyond the confines of the *Meno*, but it seems quite clear to me that, with respect to knowing, Plato affirms two things: one, human knowing is inevitably *hypothetical*; and two, hypothetical knowing is inevitably *problematic*.

And this does two things, in turn, to the right opinion-knowledge distinction. On the one hand, it underscores the methodological, rather than substantial, distinction between them; and, on the other hand, it relegates knowing to opinion, to "not-knowing," and thus underscores the openness and transcending dynamism of the human noetic process, of philosophizing itself.

A COCK TO ASCLEPIOS

INTRODUCTION

"Criton, we owe a cock to Asclepios; pay it without fail" 118a. The meaning of this command, the last made by Socrates, has not for the most part proved contentious: Socrates orders Criton to pay the debt in thankful appreciation for his immanent death which will heal his soul from its life-long and sickly affiliation with the body and sensuality.

These final words of Socrates underscore the substantial dualism of our Platonic heritage, and emphasize our responsibility, if we would be philosophers ourselves, to follow Socrates at least into the depicted separation of the noetic from the aesthetic faculties, if not all the way into death itself and life after death with its attendant rewards and punishments.

Rather than attack this interpretation head-on, I intend to "separate" literal from metaphorical expression, and ground my own quite different interpretation in a careful, differentiated reading of the dialogue, giving due attention to the literary and dramatic references connecting it to earlier and later dialogues.

The *Phaedo* is a very complex work, and is presented as the climax of the "trial trilogy"[1] which (and this will be clarified in the course of this chapter) comprises the *Apology*, the *Meno* and the *Phaedo*. So understood, the trial trilogy is devoted to the substitution of *logos* for *mythos* as the new moral paradigm. Climaxing the trilogy, the *Phaedo* develops the theme presented in Socrates' *Apology pro vita sua*, and adumbrated in the *Meno*. Socratic philosophizing is here presented as a full-fledged cultural accomplishment supplanting sophistry, traditional heroic poetry, contemporary mythic religion and natural philosophy. The structure of *logos* is delineated as erotic-hypothetical thinking, and the cultural and moral excellence of the same is paraded.

But perhaps "supplanting" is too harsh a word, for *logos* by no means vanquishes or destroys *mythos*. It is rather a question of emergence and emphasis, *logos* waxing while remaining "mixed" with *mythos*.

Regardless, the ascendancy of Philosophy presupposes a vibrant faith and trust in *logos*, the preservation of which in the defeat of misology is symbolized by the cock to be given to Asclepios, which gives this chapter its title.

Is it permitted to ask now what this command means, and to ask in such a way that our traditional accommodation of Socrates' message is challenged?

---

1 "Trial trilogy" in the context of this work. A wider assessment of Plato's philosophy would substitute the *Crito* for the *Meno* in this "trilogy".

BODY

The *Phaedo* commences with an exchange between Echecrates and Phaedon concerning the last hours of Socrates' life—"were you there yourself, Phaedon, with Socrates, or did you hear about it from someone" (57a)?—and establishes a number of parameters which we must recognize if we are to understand the message of the dialogue. First, the philosophical authenticity of the reported discussion is established. Second, the discussion is connected with Socrates' trial and sentencing (58a), and the cultural importance of attending to Socrates and his discourse is emphasized (58d). Third, Socrates is cast in the role of Theseus who saved himself and the "twice seven" from the Minotaur (58 c-d). And fourth, the theme of *mixture* is introduced (58e-59a, 60b).

In response to Echecrates' query "which of his friends were with him?" (58c), Phaedon enumerates *fourteen* specifically designated individuals:

> Of our countrymen there was this Apollodoros I have mentioned and Critobulos and his father, and, besides, Hermogenes and Epigenes and Aischines, and Antisthenes; there was also Ctesippos the Paianian and Menexenos, and others of our countrymen; but Plato was ill, I think.
> Were any foreigners present?
> Yes, Simmias the Theban and Cebes and Phaidondes; and from Megara, Eucleides and Terpsion. 59 b-c

Quite obviously, and emphatically so because Phaedon omits himself, and because the designated individuals are set off by the "and others of our countrymen", the precise enumeration of specifically indicated (thirteen by name; one by role) participants is intentional. I suggest it is intended to refer to the "twice seven" (58a) that, Phaedon tells Echecrates, the Athenians claim Theseus saved from the

Minotaur. But this is to say that *Plato is here casting Socrates in the role of Theseus.*

Dramatically, Socrates (philosophy) supplants Theseus (poetry), and we readers expectantly await the appearance of Socrates-Theseus and, anxiously, the Minotaur, the devouring beast with which Socrates-Theseus will (again) do battle.

I cannot demonstrate this casting, and I know of no argument which would convince one of the necessity of adopting the interpretation that such a casting implies. The majority of the commentators have not done so, and, in the extant literature, I have come across only one such interpretation, which I adopted with alacrity.[1] Such an interpretation does not of itself underscore the supplanting of poetry by philosophy, of *mythos* by *logos*, but lends a coherence to the dialogue which is not so apparent otherwise, and it focuses our attention on the centrality of the methodological message which neatly caps the "trial trilogy". And, lastly, it affords a "Socratic" interpretation of the ensuing discussion which skirts the "substantial" and personal-immortality interpretation which has prevailed in much of our tradition.

Personal immortality would certainly seem to be a factor in the *Phaedo*, but it is not, most emphatically, the central issue.[2] Cf. the following:

> Very well ... I will try to convince you better than I did my judges. I *believe*, my dear

---

1 Cf. Ken Dorter, *Plato's Phaedo, An Interpretation.* (Toronto: University of Toronto Press, 1982).

This is by far the most scholarly interpretation of the *Phaedo* I have read, but which--and fortunately for me--does not assign the same weight to this role-casting as I do.

2 Indeed, if Dorter is right on this score, and I believe he is, it is not even a philosophical/*logos* issue at all, but rather a religious/*mythos* issue. Dorter will insist on the centrality of *im*personal immortality.

> Simmias and Cebes, that I shall pass over first of all to other gods, both wise and good, secondly to dead men better than those in this world; and if I did not think so, I should do wrong in not objecting to death; but, *believing* this, be assured that I *hope* I shall find myself in the company of good men, *although I would not maintain it for certain;* but that I shall pass over to gods who are very good masters, be assured that *if I would maintain for certain* anything else of the kind, I would with certainty maintain this. Then for these reasons, so far from objecting, I have good *hopes* that something remains for the dead, *as has been the belief from time immemorial,* and something much better for the good than for the bad. 63 b-c (Italics added)

Is Socrates here claiming that belief in personal immortality soothes the childish fears which might otherwise assail us at the point of death? Perhaps. Cf. 77d and 114d. But perhaps there is something else here also. Note well that this statement inaugurates Socrates' defense before his new judges, and therefore we understandably assume that it has a bearing on the discussion which follows. In assessing the same, moreover, we would be ill-advised to ignore the hypothetical, fallibilistic belief-character which is emphasized repeatedly. Furthermore, shortly prior to this judicial commencement, Socrates had referred to a "tale whispered in secret," that human beings are chattel of the gods and must not take their own life, as being somewhat unreasonable—"but possibly there is a grain of reason in it" (62b). That is to say, fact and fiction (*logos* and *mythos*) are, possibly, *mixed,* inextricably interwoven, and we can untangle the two, if we can at all, only with the greatest care.

But look at the opening words of the statement again. "Very well ... I will try to convince you better than I did my judges." There can be little doubt but that this is a reference to the *Apology,* and to Socrates' defense before the Athenian judges depicted therein. Now the *Apology* is the defense of philosophy as *the noble* way of life, as the *new arete* competing with traditional and contemporary moralities for Athenian emulation. The *Apology* is not the passionate plea of an old man trying to escape execution; it is not the eloquent posturing of one trying to calculate life and death. No, most emphatically no! We ill-serve the *Apology* and ourselves if we see it as anything other than the "swan song" of philosophy, the new paradigm of human excellence.

The reference to the "judges", then, surely cannot refer simply to a calculated expectation of (personal) immortality as a device for excusing Socrates from objecting to his impending death. Rather, this reference transports us into Socrates' judicial defense of philosophy as the new *arete,* with the expectation that his defense will be more successful this time.

The discussion really gets under way with Socrates' admonition to Euenos (Cf. *Apology,* 20b) that he "follow him" as soon as possible. This elicits a guffaw from Simmias: "What advice, Socrates ... he will be the last man to obey" (61c)! To which Socrates replies simply, "Why, is not Euenos a philosopher?...but perhaps he will not do violence to himself; for they say that is not lawful" (61c).

Cebes interrupts and asks what he means by saying that philosophers will not do violence to themselves, but would be willing to follow the dying? Notice that it is Cebes who first specifies the "following" that Socrates admonishes. This occurs, most certainly, under prompting from Socrates, but his original admonition to Euenos was placed nonetheless ambiguously between his assertion that philosophy is the noblest form of poetry, and that he is about to embark on the Athenian's command.

Socrates picks up, presumably, on the physical-death interpretation of Cebes, and offers the "tale whispered in secret" that we are chattel of the gods and dare not take our own life, for it does not belong to us. To the objection that death frees us from such divine servitude, and that we ought to fear and to flee liberation from such good masters, Socrates responds: "Quite right, I think I must answer this before you as if you were a court!" (63b), and goes on to deliver the judicial statement to Simmias and Cebes I have quoted above.

A brief interruption with the jailer now occurs—Plato often introduces important new scenes with such interruptions—and Socrates launches into his defense as follows:

> Now, then, I want to give the proof at once, to you as my judges, why I think it likely that one who has spent his life in philosophy should be confident when he is going to die, and have good hopes that he will win the greatest blessings in the next world when he has ended: so Simmias and Cebes my judges, I will try to show how this could be true.
>
> The fact is, those who tackle philosophy aright are simply and solely practising dying, practising death, all the time, but *nobody sees it*. 63e-64a (Italics added)

Simmias laughs, "That's a good one for the philosophers!" (64b)—long before Freud, it seems, philosophers suffered from a death-wish—and having been found out, they richly deserve it! Notice Socrates' reply:

> That would be true, Simmias ... except the words "found out." *For they have not found out in what sense the real philosophers wish to die and deserve to die, and what kind of death it is.* 64b (Italics added.)

Attend carefully to this double insistence that nobody knows the death of which Socrates speaks. Might I deduce from this that this death is not the "normal" physical death which Socrates now picks up on by asking Simmias if he understands death as being "anything more than the separation of the soul from the body" (64c)? Socrates pursues the separation analogy and claims that the philosopher desires not bodily pleasures, indulgences and adornments, but "as far as he can stands aloof from that and turns towards the soul" (64e), to the extent that he is judged by others as not deserving to live and as being "pretty close to death" (65a).

In the pursuit of wisdom, the body so continually trips us up, the passions so distract us and the senses deceive us, that "is it not clear that in reasoning, if anywhere, something of the realities becomes visible to it" (65c)?

> And I suppose it reasons best when none of these senses disturbs it, hearing or sight, or pain, or pleasure indeed, but when it is completely by itself and says good-bye to the body, and so far as possible has no dealings with it, when it reaches out and grasps that which really is. 65c

From all of this he concludes, "genuine philosophers" (65b) come to the conclusion that the body is a continual hindrance in our pursuit of truth, and if we are ever to perceive reality we must separate ourselves entirely from it. And so, only after we are dead, and not while living-encumbered-by-the-body, shall we possess wisdom:

> For if it is impossible in company with the body to know anything purely, one thing of two follows: either knowledge is possible nowhere, or only after death ... .66e

Cebes and Simmias miss the proffered "either ... or", and eagerly pursue the image of entitative-separation, of the "purified" soul "freed from the body as if from a prison"(67d). "Those who rightly love wisdom are practising dying" (67e), and death to such is not terrifying. Indeed, fear in the face of death indicates that one is a *philosoma* rather than a *philosophia* (68b).

Courage and temperance belong to philosophers rather than, as the many believe, to the lovers-of-body, for the separation of such virtues from wisdom is mere shadow-drawing (69b; cf. the cave), and it seems that

> those who established our mystic rites were no fools; they in truth spoke with a hidden meaning long ago when they said that whoever is uninitiated and unconsecrated when he comes to the house of Hades will lie in mud, but the purified and consecrated when he goes there will dwell with gods. Indeed, as they say in the rites, 'many are called but few are chosen,' and these few are in my opinion no others than those who have loved wisdom *in the right way*. One of these I have tried to be by every effort in all my life, and I have left nothing undone according to my ability, if I have endeavored *in the right way*, if we have succeeded at all, we shall know clearly when we get there; very soon, if God will, as I think. 69 c-d (Italics added)

And the very next sentence begins "There is my defense before you gentlemen on the bench..." But one fifth through the work and we are already at the end! In one sense of the word, we are indeed at the end, and the remaining four-fifths are but clarifications and elaborations of points already stated. In another sense, however, we are far from the end, for perhaps the point of the whole work is just the clarification of points so baldly stated in Socrates' now completed *second* "apology".

Let me see if I can summarize this defense: on behalf of the Sophist Euenos, Cebes asks what Socrates has been up to composing "poetry". Socrates responds that he was but obeying a recurrent dream-command, and bids Euenos to "follow him", for he is going away at the Athenian's command. Cebes and Simmias chide him for his cavalier attitude towards death, and Socrates insists that "one who has spent his life in philosophy should be confident when he is going to die" (63e). The quest for wisdom and knowledge entails the "separation" of the noetic from the aesthetic faculties, and this is likened to the "separation" of the soul from the body which constitutes death. Therefore, and amidst heavy Orphic imagery, and since "those who tackle philosophy aright are simply and solely practising dying, practising death, all the time" (64a), the philosopher rejoices at approaching death, for only thereafter, it would seem, will he possess what he has earnestly desired all his life, reality and truth.

Cebes inaugurates the defense-sequel discussion by saying, in effect, 'fine and dandy, so long as the soul survives the death of the body'. Socrates acquiesces, and agrees to discuss "whether such a thing is *likely* or not' (70b; Italics added), that is, whether or not it is likely "that the soul exists when the man dies, and that it has some power and sense" (70b), and then refers to Aristophanes' *The Clouds* (is there irony in this reference? That is to say, is Socrates hereby indicating that he is not being serious in this discussion?) and to "the very ancient legend" (70c) that the living are continually arriving from Hades, and vice versa. But this reference to *legend* comes at the very beginning of the first argument for immortality and therefore — at least this is my contention — colors it.

Socrates proceeds to deliver three arguments for immortality: from opposition, from recollection and from invisible-analogy. The first argues for a cyclical harmonizing of opposites, with the one emerging from the other, for "if everything were combined and nothing split up, the result would be the Chaos of Anaxagoras, 'all things together'" (72c). But this is far from clear—although we should, perhaps, note its similarity to the earlier introduced concept of "mixture"—and do recall that the argued balancing of life and death characterizes not only the origin of human beings, but "of all animals and vegetables, and, in a word, everything that was birth" (70d).

What we can conclude from this, perhaps, is that the claim is made that there is a harmonizing of opposites, of life and non-life (death), with the one cyclically emerging from the other.

Nor is the second argument any less confusing. It is introduced by Cebes as "that favorite argument of yours, Socrates, which we so often heard from you" (72e), and then proceeds to enunciate *the one formal description of recollection in all of Platonic literature,* and *which is completely ignored in the argument itself.* I refer, of course, to the following:

> Then do we agree on this also, that when knowledge comes to him in such a way, it is recollection? What I mean is something like this: If a man has seen or heard something or perceived it by some other sense, and he not only knows that, but thinks of something else of which the knowledge is not the same but different, is it not right for us to say he remembered that which he thought of? 73c-d

But perhaps what is more pertinent to this argument is the insistence on the empirically-transcendent character of ideas, and the comparative evaluation which this permits (74 a-c).

I cannot let this second argument go without wondering whether or not there is irony in the very characterization Cebes gives to the argument itself. By no stretch of the imagination can we rightfully consider the argument from recollection a "favorite argument" of the *literary* Socrates! Is Plato testing, teasing us?

The third argument, purportedly designed to demonstrate post-existence of the soul rather than the pre-existence which is the focus of the first two, is offered as an antidote to the "fear which children have" that the soul is dissipated, blown-away upon the death of the body (77d). The argument proceeds from analogy: even as 'empirically-transcendent' and invisible ideas are characterized by consistency and stability when compared to material and visible shapes, so also the invisible soul is unchangeable in comparison to the changeableness of the visible and material body.

> Now you remember that we were saying some time ago that the soul, when it has the body to help in examining things, either through sight or hearing or any other sense ... is dragged by the body towards what is always changing, and the soul goes astray and is confused and staggers about like one drunken ... But when she examines by herself, she goes away yonder to the pure and everlasting and immortal and unchanging; and being akin to that, she abides ever with it, whenever it becomes possible for her to abide by herself. And there she rests from her wanderings ... .79 c-d

But this is a reference to Socrates' earlier claim that the philosopher practices dying all the time, "but nobody sees it" (63e, 67a), and it is now developed into a frankly mythical account of deserved-reincarnation (81c-82b), and into an explanation of the "deliverance and purification" conferred by philosophy (82b-d). The right loving of learning (82e) practiced by philosophy alone liberates the soul from its imprisonment in the body (82e), and alone bestows upon it that purity which allows it "communion" with divinity (83e). But this, of course, is nothing other than the supplanting of (mythic and Orphic) religion by philosophy!

"There was a long silence after Socrates had ended" (84c), and we move into the interlude in which Cebes and Simmias will present their objections which, in turn, occasion the autobiographical response from Socrates—which, I claim, contains *the* point of the whole dialogue—and the final argument and concluding myth.

Socrates breaks the long silence with his insistence that his current delivery is indeed his "swan song" (84e-85b) and that he does not regard "the present fortune a misfortune' (*ibid*).

Simmias commences, and introduces his objection with a crucial methodological consideration—this being one of the few instances in the dialogues where Plato utilizes a character other than Socrates to deliver a message of significant philosophical import (excluding, of course, the dialogues in which Socrates does not play the leading role):

> I think, as perhaps you do, Socrates, that to know the plain truth about such matters in this present life is impossible, or at least very difficult; but only a very soft man would refuse to test in every possible way what is said about them, and would give up before examining them all over till he was tired out. I think a man's duty is one of two things: either to be taught or to find out where the truth is, or if he cannot, at least to take the best possible human doctrine and the hardest to disprove, and to ride on this like a raft over the waters of life and take the risk; unless he could have a more seaworthy vessel to carry him more safely and with less danger, some divine doctrine to bring him through. 85c-d

Compare this with the following:

> for this would make us idle, and it is pleasant for soft people to hear, but our way makes them active and enquiring. 81d

This, of course, is from the *Meno*, and it is stated by Socrates immediately after his declaration that "since all nature is akin" there is nothing to hinder the enquirer from "finding out all else, if he is brave and does not weary in seeking" (81c).

Secondly, the reference to the raft on which one rides the waters of life would seem to be a direct reference to the ship in which Theseus rode the waters to Crete to do battle with the Minotaur. Can we now, then, expect to see Socrates, garbed in the armor of Theseus, battle the devouring beast, and which anticipation has been with us since the very beginning of the dialogue? Perhaps, but let us proceed cautiously.

I discount the reference to the "more seaworthy vessel" of divine doctrine on the basis of my supposition that philosophy supplants religion.

Simmias and Cebes now introduce their objections, metaphorically likening the soul to the invisible harmony of bodily parts and to the weaver of many coats who nevertheless dies and is survived by the last coat he had woven. Immediately thereupon occurs the following:

> When we had heard these two we were very unhappy, as we told one another afterwards. We had been firmly convinced by the earlier arguments, and now we seemed to be thrown back by the speakers into confusion and disbelief; we distrusted not only the earlier arguments, but those which were coming, and we thought that either we were worthless judges, or else there could be nothing to trust in the whole thing. 88c

Do you detect the shift in focus? Phaedon is no longer reporting conversations from Socrates' cell. He is now speaking directly to Echecrates about the confusion and distrust experienced by the participants to those conversations. Echecrates picks up on the shift and responds: "By heaven, Phaedon ... what argument can we trust any longer" (88d) ? Secondly, Phaedon's reference to themselves as "judges" perhaps also indicates that *the* point of *the* defense is about to be presented.

Shortly, about one-fifth of the dialogue transpiring between the two, Echecrates will again respond—and it is a definite interruption this time—and announce "Amazingly clear, as anyone with a grain of sense can see" (102a), thus concluding this particular episode. Stylistically, no other episode in the whole of the Platonic *corpus* is parenthesized as emphatically as is this one, and which I claim, contains *the* point of the *Phaedo, the* message which Plato offers us in this dialogue. But I don't claim that it is "amazingly clear" at all.

Recommencing the report, Phaedon compares Socrates to a military leader rallying his beaten troops back into battle (89a). Theseus finally makes his appearance, and we, perhaps a bit fearfully, cock our ears for the sound of the approaching Minotaur.

Socrates advises Phaedon that the two of them will cut their hair in mourning if they cannot revive the argument (89b), and that he, Phaedon, should swear an oath like the Argives not to let it grow in again until he had defeated the "two". Phaedon projects that not even Heracles could fight two. As Ioleos, then, he, Phaedon, will call in Heracles-Socrates to battle the Hydra and the Crab.

At first glance, it might appear that the Hydra and the Crab refer to Simmias' and Cebes' objections to the three arguments for immortality which have already been presented. At first glance, yes, but suspend judgement for a moment, for Socrates immediately launches into his "Don't let us be misologues" diatribe, and "the worst disease one can have is to hate arguments" (89d).

It seems to me that Plato has gone to great lengths to emphasize just this declaration. Socrates is an old man awaiting execution on a charge of impiety and corrupting young men. Pointedly, he does not bemoan his fortune. He does not decry his fate. Rather, he lordly proclaims that the very worst disease and misfortune, the very worst fate that can befall us is *the death of faith and trust in logos.* Can you not feel the hot breath scorching your neck? *Misology* is the Minotaur/Hydra with which Socrates-Heracles will do battle.

But what, then, of the Crab? Hang on.

Socrates continues his attack against misology which he claims arises, like misanthropy, from hasty, non-discriminating and over-simplifying judgements. It would be pitiable indeed to succumb to misology when perchance, there is "argument true and sound and such as can be understood" (90c-d), in the demonstration of which, Socrates assures us, he is somewhat more of a philovictor than a philosopher (91a).

He easily dispatches Simmias' objection that the soul might be nothing other than the attunement of bodily parts, and then, to the plaudits of the assembled friends, turns to Cebes' objection with the following caution:

> My good man ... don't tempt Providence, or some evil eye may overturn the argument which is coming. But God will care for that; let us charge into the fray like Homeric heroes, and try, if there's anything in your contention ... .

(Have we forgotten the heroic mold in which Socrates is cast? On the other hand, let *us* not tempt providence either; the ensuing argument *is* "overturnable". The statement continues:)

> You demand that it be proved that our soul is imperishable and immortal, if a student of philosohpy, being about to die, and being confident, and believing that after death he will be better off in that world than if he had lived to the end of a different life, is not to be found foolish and senseless in this confidence. 95 b-c

Is this, then, the point of Socrates' defense before his new judges? It is just a bit different from his earlier declaration at 63e, and "bits" are oftentimes very weighty in the dialogues. The bit in question, and I am quite willing to admit that it might be simply a question of greater emphasis, is indicated in the words "than if he had lived to the end a different life". That is to say, Socrates' defense is focused squarely on justifying philosophy as a *way of life,* and as presenting this way of life as the new model of human excellence.

Stated baldly and perhaps very awkwardly, philosophy entails the supplanting of *mythos* by *logos*. Absolutely central to the philosophic enterprise is faith and trust in *logos*. Philosophy is the antithesis of misology. And therefore, and to repeat myself, Socrates as the new Homeric hero will do battle with misology, the Minotaur and Hydra of legend. And the Crab? Why the Crab represents immortality of the soul, personal immortality. Immortality of soul is at best a peripheral issue in this dialogue. *The issue of immortality,* more specifically, *re-vivification,* is *the immortality and revivification of faith and trust in logos which vanquishes misology.*

Socrates was silent for some time after delivering himself of his interpretation of the demand laid upon him—a dramatically pregnant pause announcing germinating life—and then proclaims: "That is no trifle you seek, Cebes; we are bound to discuss generally the cause of generation and destruction" (95e).[1] He then launches into his autobiographical account arguing, in effect, that the "pre-Socratic" naturalists were illogical and empirical (and material) reductionists, and he found himself compelled to muddle along with another method of his own (97b).

Prior to delineating the same, but nevertheless already launched upon his own journey, he explains how he heard of the teaching of Anaxagoras that mind is the arranger and cause of all things, and how eagerly he sought this out, "and I thought that if this is true, mind arranging all things places everything as it is best" (97c). Unfortunately, Anaxagoras did not follow through on his promise, thinking "nothing of the good which must necessarily bind and hold all things together"

---

1 If we really are embarked upon the revivification of belief and trust in *logos*, is Socrates here telling us that such entails a new and different natural philosophy? I'm not sure, but it would not strike me as unreasonable. And, of course, there are natural philosophical overtures in the *Phaedo*, and Plato will later develop a very ambitious natural philosophy in the *Timaeus*.

(99c), and Socrates set forth on his own second sailing, his own "second voyage in search of the cause" (99c).

I suggest that Socrates' "second best voyage" (*deuteros plous)* is ironic, and is meant to recall at once the sailing of Theseus (58a) and the sailing on the raft in lieu of the more seaworthy vessel of divine doctrine which would see him safely over the turbulent waters of life (85d). The "second voyage/sailing" occurs when sailors take up their oars because the wind has died and no longer fills their sails. I have argued earlier that throughout the discussion (and in the *Meno*) Socrates attempts to 'supplant' religion (divine doctrine and myth) with philosophy. Like his earlier declaration that "formerly" he thought philosophy the highest form of poetry, so here Socrates is telling us that human beings are inveterate rowers after all, that "second best" sailing is for us the *only* sailing.

> Well then ... it occurred to me after this—and it was then I gave up contemplating the realities—that I must be careful not to be affected like people who observe and watch an eclipse of the sun... I feared that I might wholly blind my soul by gazing at practical things with my eyes and trying to grasp them by each of the senses. So I thought I must take refuge in reasoning, to examine the truth of the realities... Well anyway, this is how I set out; and laying down in each case the reasoning which I think best fortified, I consider as true whatever seems to harmonise with that, both about causes and about everything else, and as untrue whatever does not 99d-100a

and

> If anyone should attack the supposition itself, you would let him be and would not answer, until you examined the consequences to see if they were in agreement or discord together; and when you must give account of that

> supposition itself, you would do it in the same way by supposing another supposition, whichever seemed best of the higher suppositions, until you come to something satisfactory; at the same time you would not make a muddle like the dialecticians, by confusing arguments about the beginning with arguments about the consequences of the beginning, if you wished to find out something of reality ... if you are a true philosopher I believe you would do as I say. 101d-e

And *this* is "amazingly clear" according to friend Echecrates! But perhaps it is not that *un*-clear, for Socrates is claiming simply that particular statements and understandings share whatever truth-content they do from and in terms of the presuppositions sustaining them. We understand whatever it is we understand as situated within a context and pattern of relationships. The particular is conditioned by the context, and the context by a larger context, *etc.*

Unusual? It shouldn't strike us so. I suggest that such as a point of fact is indeed how we operate in each and every domain of our logical lives, and rings very true with the method followed by not a few thinkers today. In short, it is the *"logic" of the hypothetical method.*

It is here presented in a mercilessly abstract manner. But if we look at Socrates' dissatisfaction with the simple empiricism of the "natural philosophers", we can recognize the distinction between mere technique and science, between right opinion and science, as context-less and immediate affirmation on the one hand, and context-secured and therefore stable affirmation on the other. The technician and right opiner know what to do, period; but the scientist knows what to do *and why to do it,* because he places it in a larger context.

Between the two formal declarations of his "new" methodology, Socrates insists it is:

> nothing new, but the same as I have been saying all this time in our conversation, and on other occasions... the old song... supposing that there exists a beautiful something all by itself, and a good something and great and all the rest of it... 100b

—which is to say that the much touted theory of Ideas is the theory of suppositional or hypothetical thinking. *Ideas are hypotheses,* suppositions laid down in discourse as substantiating and organizing implicated statements which can be (deductively) explicated therefrom. They are supposed-contexts which stabilize and noncontradictorily integrate the particulars contained therein.

The "domain" of such ideas-hypotheses is more narrowly circumscribed in the *Phaedo* than it is in the *Meno*. In the present dialogue, the rule of ideas-hypotheses is by and large confined to discourse—"you would fear, I think that a contradictory reasoning might meet you" (101a)—and the logically-causative role is emphasized. In the *Meno,* on the other hand, the experiential role is emphasized, and the testing of the hypothesis then in question is carried out in the context of experience (empirical existence), i.e., whether or not we have ever heard or met actual teachers of virtue. The "discourse confinement" of the present hypothesizing might very well have something to do with the hypothesis of soul-immortality which is here, supposedly, in question: it is difficult to imagine how one would, during this life, experientially test such a hypothesis. Possibly, then, the present discourse-confinement of hypothetical causation is understandable. But what is more than merely possible is the absence of any attribution of ontological or entitative causation to ideas-hypotheses—in spite of the ontological role and entitative status which our tradition has assigned to Ideas.

Is all of this, then, "amazingly clear ... as anyone with a grain of sense can see" (102a)? Perhaps. But let us be clear about what is being supposed here. Socrates states that *logos* articulates a clear and coherent pattern that floats over (buoyed up by) a sea of unexamined assumptions—inevitably, for the examination of given assumptions proceeds by positing further assumptions in terms of which lower assumptions are orchestrated, "until you come to something satisfactory" (101e).

And let us also be clear about what is being stated here. Echecrates' declaration, agreed to by Phaedon "and all of them thought so who were present" (102a), is a declaration that misology has been vanquished, has been healed. It has been healed, precisely, by Socrates' "second voyage in search of the cause".

The concluding argument for immortality commences immediately after Echecrates' clarity-declaration interjection, and, in an interesting and amazingly hypothetical fashion, exemplifies the pattern here delineated.

The argument that ensues proceeds as follows: it is agreed that qualities will not admit their opposite, for upon the approach of the one the other will "either retreat or be destroyed" (102 d-e; 103d; 104b). It is then agreed that entities will not admit qualities opposite to essential-characteristics or properties of themselves. Rather, they will either retreat or be destroyed. That is to say, not only will cold not admit heat, but snow will not admit heat and fire will not admit cold. Similarly, soul will not admit death.

Having proceeded thus far with verbal contrariety, Socrates now alters his procedure and introduces *hypothetical logos*, as delineated in his "second voyage", and he does so via peculiarly anomalous analogies:

> if the uneven were necessarily imperishable, would not three be imperishable?...if the not-hot were necessarily imperishable, when someone brought a hot thing to snow the snow, would retire safe and unmelted? So also if the not-cold was brought to fire, the

> fire would not be quenched or destroyed, but it would go safe away ... And is it equally necessary to say that of the immortal? 105e-106b

He then proceeds, hypothetically, to link imperishability and immortality following the earlier agreements that three would never be even nor would fire ever be cold.

But, manifestly, such a linkage does not at all follow from, nor is it consonant with, qualitative contrariety. Rather, Socrates has posited a particular context or hypothesis, imperishability, which "contains" or "supports" immortality. It is blatantly suppositional, and Socrates treats it as such:

> So about the immortal, if we agree that this is imperishable, the soul would be imperishable as well as immortal; but if we do not, we need a new argument. 106 c-d

Cebes does not think that a new argument is needed, for "nothing could escape destruction if the immortal, which is everlasting, could be destroyed" (106d). And Socrates chimes in with "God himself and the very essence of life, and whatever else is immortal, would be admitted by all never to suffer destruction" (106d).

Socrates then asks if Simmias or anyone else has anything to say, and, in response to Simmias' admission of distrusting human weakness and of the presence of a "little incredulity" about what has been said (107b), declares:

> you are quite right, and you ought to scrutinise our first suppositions and see if you can trust them; and if you test them sufficiently, you will follow our reasoning, I think, as well as it is possible for a man to follow; and if only this be made clear, you will seek nothing further. 107b

That is to say, human reasoning is hypothetical, fallibilistic. Apodictic certitude is forever beyond our grasp and, understanding this, we "will seek nothing further." Admittedly, this last statement is tricky. Socrates either means that "first suppositions" can be *per se nota,* and therefore ground apodicticity, at which point we would "seek nothing further". Or, realizing that apodicticity belongs not to human reasoning, we will not seek or demand it at all. The first would deny the clear and emphatic assertion of Socratic not-knowing contained in the *Apology* and elsewhere. The second but serves to underscore the interpretation I am arguing here. My choice, therefore, is obvious.

But before I proceed with the concluding myth and Socrates' declaration that they owe a cock to Asclepios, like Theseus rallying his forces, let me rally my arguments before I launch my final assault.

My contention is that *the* focus of the discussion that occurred in Socrates' cell on the last day of his life has been the revivification of faith and trust in *logos* after the attack of, and in an attempt to cure, misology, "the worst disease one can have." Socrates, the new Theseus and the new Heracles, defeats the Minotaur and Hydra of misology by the tactics depicted in his "second voyage/sailing in search of the cause". The saving of himself and his companions (fourteen designated, remember) from danger, the much-touted "immortality", refers first of all to this revivification of *logos, the delineation of the proper method of which is what this dialogue is all about.*

And this *method of right reasoning* is hypothetical-*logos* erotically pursuing goodness and wisdom. The erotic pursuit of goodness, of course, is further developed in the *Symposium,* but here in the *Phaedo* hypothetical-*logos* is emphasized in precisely its conjectural and fallibilistic character: "laying down ... the reasoning which I think best fortified, I consider as true whatever seems to harmonise with that" (100a), and "by supposing another supposition, whichever seemed best of the higher suppositions, until you come to something satisfactory" (101d), and, finally, "you are quite right, and you ought still to scrutinise our first suppositions and see if you can trust them" (107b).

Socrates, decidedly, is *not* presenting us with apodictic certitude, for any claim thereof would deny his persistent declaration that human wisdom consists in knowing that one does not know, that one is not wise. Moreover, the "ideas" utilized throughout are properly understood as hypotheses suspended from/supported by "something satisfactory" which is held, primarily, on trust and, secondarily, on the basis of logical non-contradiction (*Phaedo*) and experienced non-falsification (*Meno*).

I cannot emphasize too much that Socrates' *logos* is nowhere *per se nota;* it nowhere rests on absolute certitude, clarity and distinctness. What? Is Plato not a philosopher? Rather, perhaps, we philosophers have forgotten what it is to be philosophers (lovers of wisdom), i.e., out of our own acknowledged not-knowing erotically to pursue knowing *via* the hypothetical method. Such at least would seem to be the import of this dialogue, Socrates' "swan song".

But perhaps the "something satisfactory" still haunts us. Indeed it should. I refer you to Julias Elias' recent study, *Plato's Defense of Poetry*,[1] wherein it is argued, quite successfully I think, that the "something satisfactory", the "key stone" in the arch of hypothetical *logos*, is posited allegorically in various myths and legends—and in various kinds of myths and legends, running the gamut from the myth of Er to the *Timaeus*, from the hypothetical method of knowing postulated in the "second voyage" of the *Phaedo* to the allegory of the line of the *Republic*.

---

1 Julius Elias, *Plato's Defense of Poetry* (London: Macmillan Press, 1984).

I have argued that the new *arete* represented by Socrates consists in the supplanting of *mythos* by *logos*. I don't deny it. But, ultimately, this *logos* is suspended from/supported by *mythos*, from *mythos* which must be delineated conceptually and tested experientially. Ultimately, *logos* is indeed suspended from a supposition, and this very suspension must be clarified conceptually, systematized and tested experientially. It is these latter logical and rational steps which enable us to sort the "mixing" and orchestrate the chaos of Anaxagoras. And this unified operation of understanding, reasoning or philosophy, is itself a mixture of *mythos* and *logos* (dare I call it "conjectures and refutations"?). Fact and fancy, soul and body are mixed—we cannot forget that Plato presents Socrates at the beginning and end of this dialogue accompanied by, mixed with, his wife and children—the most "spiritual" of heroes is presented as a sexual and biologically-responsive individual—and it is erotically-motivated *hypothetical logos* which justifies philosophy as the new model of human excellence.

Suspended from *mythos*? Yes, and Socrates now launches into the "myth of the variegated earth" which, in effect, crowns the arguments for immortality. Apart from the biological-cosmological themes posited therein (and which will be clarified and systematized in the *Timaeus*), and the judgement and consequent rewards and punishments of the surviving souls, the more hypothetical-*logos*-pertinent *mythos* is perhaps contained in the depiction of the mist-filled hollows human beings inhabit, surmounted by the highlands of purity and beauty of the true earth and heaven (shades of the Cave!).

> No sensible man would think it proper to rely on things of this kind just as I have described; but that, since the soul is clearly immortal, this or something like this at any rate is what happens in regard to our souls and their habitations—that this is so seems to me proper and worthy of the risk of believing, for the risk is noble. 114 d

Socrates admonished his friends to take care of themselves "following the footsteps, so to speak, of both this last conversation and those we have had in former times" (115b), bathed, talked to his family, offered a libation to the gods "for good luck in the migration from here to there" (117c), and drank the potion. He addressed his final words to his friend, Criton: "We owe a cock to Asclepios; pay it without fail" (118a).

Bear with me as I insist, for the last time, that this thank-offering to the god of healing is more-than-probably offered in gratitude for the healing from misology effected by Socrates' erotically-motivated, second-voyage hypothetical-*logos*.

Phaedon concludes the dialogue:

> This was the end of our comrade, Echecrates, a man, as we would say, of all then living we had ever met, the most noble and the wisest and the most just. 118a

CONCLUDING REMARKS

An earlier version of this essay[1] prompted a request for clarification of "soul" in the *Phaedo*. By way of concluding this rather lengthy interpretation, I will attempt to outline such a clarification.

My initial supposition is that "soul", i.e., the human soul, denotes the behavior of Socrates. What "soul" connotes is precisely the point of the explicatory-exercise that the *Phaedo* is all about.

---

1 The earlier version was delivered at Colby College, the University of Maine, Spring 1985, and the specific request came from the commentator, Professor Francis H. Parker, and to whom I would like to pay my own thank-offering for the critical encouragement he offered.

(Human) soul primarily refers to the erotic-logical behavior exemplified by Socrates. That is to say, soul primarily is hypothetical thinking. Biological soul, the organic-perceptual functionings of *bios,* is subsidiarily constitutive of the specifically distinctive human soul. *The* focus of the *Phaedo* is the explication of the specifically distinctive human soul rather than the subsidiarily constitutive *bios* implicated therein. And this specifically distinctive human soul, to repeat myself, is thinking, erotic-hypothetical-*logos.*

"Soul" is an acting; it is human believing/thinking, and anything and everything that this implies. It is, decidedly, not a *substance,* not a "spiritual entity". Admittedly, this is not how we have interpreted "soul" in Plato. But our traditional bias does not, of itself, say anything about what Plato might be trying to say to us about soul as erotic-logical behavior.

The explication of such behavior is the focus of the *Phaedo,* and it is carried out *via* a two-pronged attack: one, through the elaboration of a precise thesis—erotic-hypothetical-*logos* is the new pattern of human excellence as exemplified in Socrates' "second voyage in search of the cause", and, two, through the re-presentation and re-enactment of the (Poetic) battles of Theseus and Heracles now presented as the battle of Socrates to introduce this new pattern in the face of historic and contemporary opposition. In short, it is the battle to supplant *Mythos* by *Logos.*

While the resulting battle is, admittedly, confusing, the underlying pattern of assault is quite clear. It is the way of right thinking, the way of erotically-motivated hypothetical-logic. And this, of course, is what the human soul is. It *is* the erotic-erruption, the hypothetical reaching-out-towards "something satisfactory", the beautiful and the good, standing on which alone we will "clearly", "definitively" and "systematically" know and understand.

Such definitive understanding is the goal towards which the soul is the striving, towards which the soul is the reaching out without ever, finally, grasping. But such self-overreaching is nothing other than erotically-motivated hypothetical-thinking, the positing of context-supported-particulars and of context-supporting conditioned - contexts, *etc*. And this hypothesizing *is* idealizing, idea-izing, for ideas are hypotheses, clarifying and integrating suppositions.

The intimacy between Ideas and the human soul is emphasized throughout the Platonic corpus. It is usually depicted in a memorably graphic and mythical manner. The "sneak-previewing" of Ideas in the *Phaedrus* is particularly impressive, and emphasizes, among other things, that only souls that have previewed Ideas are capable of becoming human souls.

That such intimacy is indeed characteristic of souls is, of course, correct. But we have fallen short of the challenge Plato throws down to us in this depiction to the extent that we have accepted its mythic and symbolic representation literally. I see very little support in the dialogues for our traditional reification of Ideas, nor for any literal interpretation of knowledge as recollection.

Plato, rather, is arguing that humans, like Socrates, do not know and desire to know; we operationalize this desire by laying-down clarificatory/explanatory guesses in a successively-conditioned hierarchicalization, the ultimate goal of which is full understanding of the human situation.

The project is suppositional throughout, but checked by its insistence on conceptual clarity and consistency, and experiential relevance and viability. In short, it is hypothetical-knowing, erotically-motivated hypothetical-*logos*.

It is this soul as the hypothetical-knowing-project-itself which is progressively clarified in the dialogues, and is presented as the new model and pattern of human excellence. Nor is such clarification-presentation a simple matter, for it is carried out in the throes of cultural and political battles with Socrates' enemies; with those who executed him, and with those who make claims upon human knowing which, on the one hand (the Sophists and empiricists), belittle the powers of human knowing, and, on the other hand (Religionists and politicians), overpass its powers in their claims of certitude and infallibility.

Is, then, this "soul" immortal? That is to say, will this self-transcending-hypothetical-knowing personally survive the death of the body? With Socrates, I honestly don't know. I am not even sure that I, *or Socrates,* consider this a philosophically-relevant question. This has not of course been our traditional response, but then our traditional interpretation of the *Phaedo* has not properly appropriated Socrates' "conversations" (115b). And we have not done so because we have insisted on a literal interpretation of Socrates' metaphorical discourse.

But this brings me back to the beginning of my essay, and completes the circle.

THE SYMPOSIUM

The culturally dramatic setting of the *Symposium* is, again, of utmost importance if we are to understand the revolutionary intention of Plato's message. But because this setting is similar to what we have already seen, I will not repeat my setting-delineation here—but for one small point, a dramatic setting introduced for the first time in this dialogue, and repeated shortly in the *Republic*.

I refer to the setting of transience, of being-on-the-way towards a destination that is introduced with the opening words of Apollodoros and repeated at the conclusion of his introductory remarks: "... I was coming up to town ..." and "... the road to town will do well enough for us to talk and listen as we go."

Interspersed between the *viator* remarks, and recalling the previous conversation with Glaucon, Apollodoros emphasizes his imitation of Socrates in his earnest attempt to be a philosopher. Indeed, he concludes his proem with an encomium on Philosophy:

> The truth is that whenever I speak about philosophy myself or hear others doing so, I am highly delighted, besides believing that it does me good. But when I hear other kinds of talk, especially among you rich men and moneymakers, it annoys me, and I pity you,

> my friends, because you are doing nothing while you think you are doing something. 173 c-d

But this is to situate philosophy *on-the-road, on the way towards* a destination while never quite reaching it. Philosophy is a journey. It is, of course, Socratic not-knowing, but now presented, as will shortly become apparent in the dramatic working-out of the dialogue, in the context of the dynamics of *Eros* rather than in the dynamics of *Logos*, such as we were presented in the *Phaedo*. Even as the *Phaedo* presents the dynamics of ascending-Logos, so the *Symposium* presents the dynamics of ascending-*Eros*.. They are, in fact, the two sides of the one coin. And this on-the-road dynamics is peculiarly reminiscent of Heraclitus. The *Symposium* must be understood as a journey with Heraclitus in an attempt to *understand* dynamics.

Fully half of the *Symposium* is devoted to Socrates, itself rather neatly divided into Socrates' Diotima-speech and Alcibiades' Socrates-speech. The first delineates the structure of *Eros* itself, and the second demonstrates the incarnation and instantiation of the same in the person and behavior of Socrates. Once again, Socrates is presented center-stage as the model of cultural and human excellence, and in such a manner as to turn upside-down traditional and contemporary models. But the core of Plato's message is contained in Socrates' Diotima-delineation of the structural dynamism of the erotic ascent itself.

Socrates commences his dissertation by commending Agathon on his "fine Gorgias-like speech, and then chides the assembled men for contenting themselves with "seemings" rather than truth:

> I make no eulogy in this fashion: I could not do it. However, the truth, if you like: I have no objection to telling the truth, in my own fashion. Will you listen to the truth being told about Love, in any words and arrangement of phrases such as we may hit on as we go? 199a-b

Remember, now, that when Eryximachos first proposed that they entertain themselves with declamations of *Eros*, Socrates exclaimed "No one will vote against you .... I could not refuse myself, I suppose, when love is the only thing I profess to know about" (177e). Is this not an unusual declaration for the *not-knowing* Socrates to make? Perhaps, but perhaps not, if indeed *Eros* is not so much a thing or destination as it is the *journey towards* a destination. Anyway, here in his apology to the assembled "experts", Socrates contents himself with noting the difference of his nonrhetorical declamation of *Eros*.

He proceeds to elicit from Agathon an agreement that *Eros*, being a striving-and-reaching-out-towards, lacks the perfections towards which it strives and which traditionally have been attributed to it. Agathon's earlier speech is contradicted, then, even as an earlier declamation of Socrates was contradicted later in exchanges between himself and Diotima—"And she it was who taught me about love affairs" (202a).

Even as in Socrates' exchange with Agathon, Diotima convinced Socrates that *Eros* is neither beautiful nor good. Nor is it ugly or bad. Rather, even as "right opinion" (202a) is between wisdom and ignorance, so *Eros* is "something between" (202b) beautiful and ugly. *Eros* is a great spirit, between the divine and the mortal, carrying the messages of the one to the other, "and being in the middle it completes them and binds all together into a whole" (202e). *Eros* is Philosophy!

In response to Socrates' query "What use is he to mankind?" Diotima clearly states that the love of obtaining beauty and good is constitutive of human nature. But this love is *Eros*. *Eros*, ,then, is constitutive of the very being of human beings as such. That is to say, ontologically we are on-the-way, reaching-out towards wisdom, beauty and good, the capture and possession of which would be happiness.

And because such capture and possession lies forever beyond our mortal reach, Diotima further specifies the *Eros* in question:

> Socrates, love is not for the beautiful, as you think... . It is for begetting and birth in the beautiful... Because begetting is, for the mortal, something everlasting and immortal. 206e

Here Plato introduces a most important *ontological characteristic* of mortal being: *mortal life seeks immortality.* Mortality *is* the seeking-after and reaching-out-towards immortality. Mortality is the process of constantly over-reaching itself.

> the mortal is preserved, not by being wholly the same always, like the divine, but because what grows old and goes leaves behind something new like its past self. By this device, Socrates, ... mortality partakes of immortality, both in body and in all other respects; but it cannot otherwise. 208a-b

Mortality *is* the process of constantly over-reaching *and falling-short-of* itself. Mortality is on-the-road, it is the very process itself of being-on-the-road without ever reaching the destination towards which it is travelling.

Perhaps the traditional distinction between Being and Becoming will help us understand Diotima's message. But I want to focus on the distinction a little differently than has been our custom. The text is quite clear, I think, that Diotima is here characterizing Heraclitean Becoming, and stating that the whole realm of organic and human life can be understood only as the tragic-comic attempt of Becoming to appropriate Being. Becoming is the 'eternal-return of over-reaching/falling-short, the endless being-on-the-road of the reproductively-cyclic pursuit of permanence:

> Consider that for a while each single living creature is said to live and to be the same; for example, a man is said to be the same from boyhood to old age; he has, however, by no means the same things in himself, yet he is

> called the same: he continually becomes new, though he loses parts of himself, hair and flesh and bones and blood and all the body. Indeed, not only body, even in soul, manners, opinions, desires, pleasures, pains, fears, none of these remains the same, but some perish and others are born. And far stranger still, this happens to knowledge too; not only do some kinds of knowledge perish in us, not only are other kinds born, and not even in our knowledge are we ever the same, but the same happens even in each single kind of knowledge. For what is called study and practice means that knowledge is passing out; forgetting is knowledge leaving us, and study puts in new knowledge instead of that which is passing away, and preserves our knowledge so that it seems to be the same. 207d-208a

The specifically human pursuit of permanence presents itself more in people who are "pregnant in soul" (209a) than in those "pregnant in body". To this class belong the poets, artists and craftsmen, and especially the law-givers demonstrating justice and temperance (209a-b) who 'live-on' in the institutions and cities they have founded (209d).

It is no exaggeration to say that tragedy predominates in this depiction of Becoming. The passing-away and death that characterizes living organisms renders permanence vicarious at best. Nor is it any better in the more human and cultural dimension, for Socrates at least is bent on supplanting his predecessors and radically transforming Hellenic culture, artistic and political.

So tragedy reigns, and not only inasmuch as each of us eventually dies, but because we are dying throughout our life. Permanence and identity are denied us even in the course of our life. Does this loss of personal identity recall Socrates' opening words in the *Apology*? There he "almost forgot who he was," and here permanence and (personal) identity is relegated beyond our reach, and but vicariously approachable only through the continual change and becoming of reproduction.

Is it for such reasons, perhaps, that Diotima introduces her most important qualifications as she launches into the second part of her dissertation? And if the first can be called tragic, the second can perhaps be called comic, for herein she grapples with the question of relative and comic permanence and identity in an overall tragic-comic depiction of human life.

> These are some of the mysteries of Love,Socrates, in which perhaps even you may become an initiate; but as for the higher revelations, which initiation leads to if one approaches in the right way, I do not know if you could ever become an adept. At least I will instruct you ... and no pain will be lacking; you try to follow if you can. 209e-210a

A number of points in this statement should catch our attention. The first is that this philosophical pursuit of *Eros* is presented in decidedly religious dress. This but indicates the culturally revolutionary force of Socrates' supplanting of religion by philosophy which I have already emphasized. The second, and again this has been presented earlier in both the *Meno* and the *Phaedo*, is the emphasis placed on method, on the "right way". And third *and most important*,, the point is made that Socrates will *not* understand the "higher revelations". No effort will be spared on Diotima's part, but *Socrates will not understand*.

This is a most crucial declaration, and if we fail to understand it, we will fail to understand what the *Symposium* is all about. Socrates is on the way towards understanding, and he will fail to reach his goal. Understanding lies beyond the reach of Socrates! But Socrates is *the* model of human excellence. The humanly excellent, then, is on the way towards understanding, and on the way towards goodness, beauty, permanence and identity *without ever reaching its destination*. Socratic not-knowing prevails. Tragedy triumphs.

But this was indicated earlier in the dialogue when Socrates arrived late from his mystical encounter *with nothing to say*. Indeed, he chided Agathon for his simplistic assumption that wisdom could pass between men through the rubbing of shoulders:

> If wisdom is like that, I think it precious to be beside you, for I think I shall be filled up with fine wisdom. Mine would be poor stuff and questionable, like a dream 175d

But tragedy does not triumph completely. Perhaps the dream saves us, or at least the *right way* of advancing through the journey that is life will confer upon us a semblance of the identity, immortality and happiness which is the goal of human living.

Diotima now launches into what I call her ascensional-analysis of *Eros*, of the philosopher or the excellent human being. The right way of living of human life is ascending through the four levels of beauty, from attention to the one beautiful body at the bottom to the one knowledge and science of Beauty at the top.

But let us not be too hasty. The ascension, first of all, must be seen to be a *cumulative* ascent, rather than a simple leaving behind that which we have ascended beyond. This is emphasized repeatedly, albeit indirectly, in the particular situations in which Socrates is depicted in the dialogue: he is 'attracted to' the physical beauty of Agathon and Alcibiades, and he does not shy away from banquets and from consuming vast quantities of wine; he is given to mystical contemplation and physical toughness. But the ascension is truly an ascending—one must not remain stuck on one level, as Alcibiades does. Secondly, the ascension is clearly presented as responding to the appeal and the allure of beauty, of transcendent Beauty which instances itself "in" the lower orders and draws us progressively up and through these orders to the "last grade" (210e), the fourth and highest level. And thirdly, and keeping in mind the ignorance and impotence which Diotima introduced with her "higher revelations", this fourth level is not so much invaded as indicated as the goal towards which Socrates and we are travelling. It is the intersection towards which converging lines point, but without ever reaching. I will return to this.

Diotima, then, describes three levels through which *Eros* proceeds as it heads towards the fourth. The first is the realm of physical beauty, intercourse with which generates beautiful speech. The second is the realm of cultural and psychic beauty, intercourse with which generates "such talks as will make young people better" (210c). Together, these realms are described as "practice" (210c), and the movement through and above these as the movement into "knowledge". The realm of knowledge is also divided into two. The first, the third in the order of ascent, is the realm of many intelligent disciplines, of the many intellectual disciplines, presumably, then present in Athens and Hellas. Plato does not specify them, and contents himself with declaring that intercourse with such will "give birth to many beautiful and magnificent speeches and thoughts in the abundance of philosophy . . ." (210d).

Diotima concludes her brief description of third-level "contemplation" with reference to the "one knowledge, the one science of this beauty now to be described" (210d)—and then proceed to offer us no description at all!

> Suddenly he will behold a beauty marvellous in its nature, that very Beauty, Socrates, for the sake of which all the earlier hardships had been born: in the first place, everlasting, and never being born nor perishing, neither increasing nor diminishing; secondly, not beautiful here and ugly there, not beautiful now and ugly then, not beautiful in one direction and ugly in another direction, not beautiful in one place and ugly in another place. Again, this beauty will not show itself

> to him like a face or hands or any bodily thing at all, nor as a discourse or a science, nor indeed as residing in anything as in a living creature or in earth or heaven or anything else, but being by itself with itself always in simplicity 210e-211b

The Parmenidean overtones of this "description" are quite unmistakable, but I think we would be very mistaken to focus our attention upon them. No. What is even more pronounced in this "description" is that it is no description at all! It is *negative theology* at its best. The Beautiful and the Good, that towards which all life and especially human life aims, is not this and it is not that, it is not here and it is not there. It is transcendent and ineffable, and yet it is that towards which organic life, and especially human life, is on-the-way because it attracts every living thing towards itself. Life *is* a being-on-the-way towards... . Life *is* a self-transcending movement beyond itself into... . Life *is* a pointing beyond itself towards... . But towards what, and into what?

> What indeed ... should we think, if it were given to one of us to see beauty undefiled, pure, unmixed, not adulterated with human flesh and colors and much other mortal rubbish, and if he could behold beauty in perfect simplicity? 211e

But of course this is precisely what is not given to us, and will never be given to us so long as we live! Mortal rubbish *is* the trappings of human life, and let us not forget Socrates' characterization of human wisdom in the *Apology* that it is worth little or nothing.

Again,

> Do you not reflect ... that there only it will be possible for him, when he sees the beautiful with the mind, which alone can see it, to give birth not to likeness of virtue, since he touches no likeness, but to realities, since he touches reality; and when he has given birth

> to real virtue and brought it up, will it not be granted him to be the friend of God, and immortal if any man ever is? 212a

Negative and mystical theology from the mouth of a prophetess—but not knowledge, and not any description of a human milieu, however lofty we might imagine the reaches of human nature. No, Diotima's "perfect secret" (211b) is beyond human nature. It is that towards which human excellence points, that towards which human life nobly lived *is* a pointing. It is the self-overreaching, the "right approach" which confers upon human life and nature a "comic" and "dream" identity and permanences, the only identity and permanence open to us.

But this is not at all to deny that such comic and dream status has any existential and cultural impact. Indeed, Alcibiades' Socrates-speech which follows immediately underscores precisely the "solidity" of Socrates' personality and behavior, and the impact it had on him, and can have on us.

As I indicated earlier, Plato devotes approximately one-quarter of the whole dialogue to Alcibiades' Socrates-speech. It plays a major part in the *Symposium,* and it behooves us to under-stand it carefully if we would understand what the *Symposium* is telling us.

The first point, then, is that Alcibiades' speech is a direct response to Eryximachos' instruction that he should deliver himself of an "eulogy in honor of Love" (241c). Alcibiades responds that Socrates will not permit him to praise anybody, "god or man other than himself" (241d) in his presence. Very well, then, Eryximachos now instructs him, "praise Socrates" (214d). *But this is to cast Socrates in the role of Eros*! And Alcibiades will now go on and demonstrate that the behavior of Socrates exemplifies, step by step, the "right way" of the ascent to the Beautiful that is *Eros* as delineated in Socrates' Diotima speech.

Alcibiades commences by insisting, much after the fashion of Socrates earlier in the dialogue, that he will tell the truth, so much as he is able, "for it is not easy to set out all your absurdities nicely in order, for one in my state" (215a). We wonder whether Alcibiades' confusion lies more in his intoxication from the "absurdities" and paradoxical behavior of Socrates-*Eros* than it does in his intoxication from the quantity of wine that he has already consumed.

Regardless, Alcibiades is forced to utilize similes to capture the slippery Socrates, and compares him to Silenos, Marsyas, a bully and a piper. But this is to say that Socrates has a decided impact upon others, indeed an "intoxicating" impact that draws people above themselves and elicits "shame" (216b) that they are content to remain at lower levels, beneath themselves and their possibilities.

Throughout, Alcibiades lauds Socrates' attraction to physical beauty and his physical powers, his cultural and social accomplishments and talents, his intellectual and logical skills and, finally, his mystical rapture (220c).

Socrates is unique:

> One could quote many other things in praise of Socrates, wonderful things: of his other habits one might perhaps say much the same about another man, and yet it is not his being like any other man in the world, ancient or modern, that is worthy of all wonder. Men like Achilles might be found, one might take, for example, Brasidas and others; and again men like Pericles, such as Nestor and Antenor, and there are more besides; and so we might go on with our comparisons. But as for this man, so odd, both the man and his talk, none could ever be found to come near him, neither modern nor ancient ... 221c-d

The final laudation is reserved for Socrates' talk—even his talk is very like the opening Silenoses:

> When you agree to listen to the talk of Socrates, it might seem at first to be nothing but absurdity; such words and phrases are wrapped outside it, like the hide of a boisterous satyr ... 221d

Socrates is *Eros* incarnate. But Socrates also is the paradigmatic human being. In Socrates we witness the pattern and the meaning of what it is to be human. To be nobly human, then, is to be *Eros* incarnate, it is to imitate and exemplify the erotic ascent to the Beautiful so manifest in the behavior and person of Socrates.

Human nature is a sign pointing beyond itself. We are on-the-way-towards a transcendent and ineffable destination which forever remains beyond our reach, but the very pursuit of which consolidates us in the only identity and permanence which is open to us in the Heraclitean process in which we find ourselves.

Human life is the tragic-comic pursuit of Beauty and Goodness responding to the allure of this selfsame Beauty and Goodness acting upon us in the depths of our souls. Our response is our journeying-upwards, perpetually over-reaching ourselves, without, however, reaching any destination. Human life remains on-the-way, a tragic-comic pursuit of self-overcoming which works out its own identity and permanence by responding "in the right way" to this Transcendent which forever eludes it.

It is by way of responding to the dynamics of such a transient life that Socrates concludes the *Symposium* with his insistence to the tragedean Agathon and the comedian Aristophanes that the same man ought to understand how to compose both comedy and tragedy, and that he who has skill as a tragic poet has skill for a comic poet. 223d

THE *REPUBLIC*
OR
SPELIOLOGICAL RE-ALIGNMENT

The *Republic* is generally considered Plato's *magnum opus,* his utopian masterpiece which has spawned a succession of imitations and which definitively underscores the political and social importance of (Plato's) philosophy. Untold generations of young philosophers have cast themselves in the role of the Philosopher King, and though democracy does not fare too well under such tutelage, the politically-directive role of knowledge is clearly indicated, if only "idealistically" and in the "City in words".

Generally speaking, the *Republic* has been interpreted rather literally, and we have not hesitated, we democrats, to see delineated therein a noble pattern of education and the definitive articulation of Plato's "epistemology" and "metaphysics". It would be impossible to calculate the damage that such a too-simplistic reading of the *Republic* has done to young minds!

While Plato is not a simplistic writer, he is not a terribly difficult writer either. And while he is not an easy read, he is not misleading—if we are attentive to the cues he offers us. The very first cue, perhaps, that should tune us into the message of the *Republic* is the absolute incongruity that exists between Socrates as he is usually depicted in the dialogues and the Philosopher King. Socrates does not know and knows that he does not know, while the Philosopher King is an infallible and insufferable expert, if ever there was one. And can any of us even imagine Socrates manipulating and controlling people *via* a "noble lie" such as is central to the regime herein described? No, no, the *Republic* is *not* to be interpreted literally!

Almost two decades ago John Herman Randall, Jr., in his *Plato, Dramatist of the Life of Reason* (New York & London: Columbia University Press, 1970), warned us of such a too-literal reading, and offered instead an ironic reading such that the *Republic* becomes a *reductio ad absurdum* of Protagorean politicizing and Spartan law-and-order, in an attempt by Plato, perhaps, to subvert Sophistic and Doric support in defeated Athens.

And recently Mary P. Nichols in her *Socrates and the PoliticalCommunity, An Ancient Debate* (Albany: State University of New York Press, 1987) shares with us a similar warning, but now identifying the *Republic* as a caricature of Aristophanes' *The Clouds,* wherein Plato argues that extreme and simplistic politics are just as destructive of the *Polis* as Aristophanes claims that Socratic philosophizing is. Indeed, it is even more destructive.

In my own reading of the *Republic* I have shied away from the conventionally literal interpretation through the use of two devices: one, a conscious and consistent recall of the paradigmatic and fallibilistic Socrates as delineated especially in the *Apology,* and two, a selective reading of the *Republic,* focusing mainly on the three central allegories of the Sun, the Line and the Cave.

The following essay utilizes these devices, and is not therefore to be considered an interpretation of the *Republic* as a whole, but does touch base, I hope, with what I understand to be one of its central themes: the delineation of the erotic, fallibilistic *logos* as the very structure and meaning of human life and being.

Recall the setting of the allegories. Socrates has been discussing with Adeimantos and Glaucon the absolute importance of political leaders possessing knowledge of the good. Leaders must possess a 'bright, shining pattern' of the good in their soul else they will not be leaders at all! The two agree, and in response to Adeimantos' query, "But what do you say yourself, Socrates? Is knowledge the good, or pleasure, or something else?" (506b), Socrates offers a metaphor or allegory of the good, on the basis that it is not fair "for a man to speak about what he doesn't know as if he does" (506c).

It is very important that we understand the dynamics of this exchange. Socrates has convinced his interlocutors of the necessity of knowledge of the good for leadership. But when pressed as to what the good is, he pleads ignorance:

> I fear my present impulse is not strong enough to carry me as far as what I think on that subject now. 506e

Paul Shorey's translation is even more suggestive:

> let us dismiss for the time being the nature of the good in itself, for to attain to my present surmise of that seems a pitch above the impulse that wings my flight today.

Socrates pointedly insists that his discourse *falls short of* the good. But

> there is an interesting offspring of the good, as it seems to me, and very like it; I am willing to speak of that... I only wish... that I could pay it up and you two could pocket the whole, and not merely the off-spring interest as now. Anyway, put in your pockets this interest and offspring of the good itself; only be careful that I may not cheat you and myself by paying spurious coin in the account. 506e-507a

He than proceeds to deliver himself of the three metaphors or allegories of the Sun, the Line and the Cave.

THE ALLEGORY OF THE SUN

> Surely, now ... my meaning must appear to be that this, the offspring of the good which the good begat, is in relation to the good itself an analogy, and what the good effects, by its influence, in the region of the mind, towards mind and things thought, this the sun effects in the region of seeing, towards sight and things seen. 508b-c

Rather than a Plotinian ontological-emanationist theme which is often associated with this allegory, its focus is towards an analogical explanation of intelligibility by comparing it with visibility. Even as actual sight and actual visibility are bathed in light, and are therefore the issue as it were of the sun as the source of light, so also actual understanding and actual intelligibility are bathed in the "light" of the good. Now the good is that towards which we strive, by which we orient ourselves. And this, then, is to say that actual understanding with its concomitant meaning and intelligibility is a function of ultimate orientation, is integrated with the ultimate goal towards which we are heading, whatever that might be.

Remember that we are discussing *leaders*, and here Socrates is simply stating that effectiveness of leadership is dependent upon connecting leadership with attunement with the goal and end of the leadership in question. Whoever knows where they are going can effectively utilize the intermediate steps so that they can proceed towards their goal. Whoever does not know where they are going is fated to walk in circles. The goal, therefore, integrates and grounds the particulars organized by it. And the good, the ultimate focus of human experience, integrates and grounds everything which falls within human experience.

The good, then, confers intelligibility upon whatever falls within its range as organized by it. But the good itself is not thereby understood. It remains beyond intelligibility and understanding.

Because intelligibility seems largely synonymous with reality for Plato, the traditional ontological interpretation of the allegory of the Sun does not seem to be entirely wide of the mark. I have reservations, however, when such is developed into an entitative-emanationist schema, and the good is interpreted as a quasi-divine and even creative ground of creaturehood. Retrospection does indeed sometimes get the better of us.

But when all is said and done, Plato's allegory of the Sun is consistently abstract and formal. There is nothing "substantial" about it—indicated perhaps in Glaucon's closing exclamation: "O Lord, what a devil of a hyperbole!" (509c)

THE ALLEGORY OF THE LINE

The second allegory, the allegory of the Line, follows immediately, and is introduced by an exchange which indicates that the level of discussion has risen to a higher plane, and that—I claim, anyway—it is the most significant of the three allegories:

> Oh, please don't stop! ... At least do finish the comparison with the sun, if you are leaving anything out.
> Oh yes ... I am leaving a lot out.
> Not one little bit, please!
> I'm afraid I must leave out a great deal ... *but I won't willingly leave out anything now if I can help it.* 509c (Italics added)

And now Socrates introduces the Line.

> Suppose you take a line, cut into two unequal parts to represent in proportion the worlds of things seen and things thought, and then cut each part in the same proportion. Your two parts in the world of things seen will differ in degree of clearness and dimness, and one part will contain images; by images I mean first of all shadows, then reflections in water and in surfaces which are of close texture, smooth and shiny and everything of that kind ...
>
> Take the second part of this for the things which the images resemble, the animals about us and all the trees and plants and all kinds of manufactured articles ...
>
> Now then, consider how the section for things thought should be divided .... . In the first part the soul in its search is compelled to use as images the things imitated—the realities of the former part—and from things taken for granted passes not to a new beginning, a first principle, but to an end, a conclusion; in the second part it passes from an assumption to a first principle free from assumption, without the help of images which the other part uses, and makes its path of enquiry amongst ideals themselves by means of them alone. 509e-510b

Again, this must be seen as more of an epistemological than as an ontological-entitative allegory. It is important that we attend to the *one* line permeating the four levels here depicted. Human knowing is *one,* with differing degrees of darkness and light, of confusion and clarity. The human world, correspondingly, is *one,* variously interpreted and epistemically structured.

The Line depicts the ascent of knowing through sensibility to intelligibility, through the "I see it" to the "I know it". But what is absolutely crucial about this ascent—and which, unfortunately, has not always been picked up by students of Plato—is the *cross-over* from 'objective' representation on the sensible level to 'subjective' and methodological representation on the intelligible level.

The only entitative-substantial objects indicated in this allegory lie on the second level, what Plato calls "belief". They are the natural and artificial things we find about us. They are the independent objects of sensation. The images and reflections of the first level are dependent-sensibles, dependent objects of sensation, immediately indicative of their entitative progenitors, the physical objects of the second level which cast them as shadows and reflections. We cannot rest on the first level, for the dependent-sensibilities refer us beyond themselves to the independent-sensibilities of belief.

The bottom two levels of the Line, then, indicate the entitative-objects of sensibility, and there is suggested an emanative-productive relationship holding between them such that the one, the second, "produces" the other, the first, these being related as entitative model and image.

But human beings at least cannot rest content with pure sensation. Inevitably we interpret and try to understand what we see. We identify and relate sensible objects in a cultural endeavor to make sense of our situation.

And it is this specifically human exercise of understanding and intellectual activity which is the focus of the Line. Plato insists that there are two levels of intellectual activity operating in such an exercise. On the one hand, there is that level or type of understanding (what Plato called *dianoia)* which correlates and interprets data in terms of unexamined assumptions and suppositions. "Unexamined" is the key word here. On the other hand, there is that intellectual activity which critically investigates and examines the assumptions and suppositions themselves, straining towards a suppositionless beginning, a *per se nota,* which would ground all subsequent suppositions, conferring upon them that infallibility and solidity which characterizes "knowledge". Plato calls this level and type of understanding "exercise of reason", *noesis.*

It is important that we appreciate that *reasoning* is for Plato vectorial; it is what is indicated as pointed-out and presupposed by the dianoetic understanding that is the normal and third level intellectual activity. It is nowhere indicated that human beings can attain such an absolute intuition. Socrates most certainly did not. But who among us can refrain from imagining the inclining slopes of the mountain we are climbing converging at the peak? We do not stand on this peak, and we cannot even see it there in the clouds above us. But we imagine it. It must be there, for the inclining slopes indicate a convergence up ahead.

Dianoetic, third-level understanding proceeds by way of *hypotheses,* by way of laying-down assumptions or suppositions from which conclusions are deduced. Dianoetic understanding does *not* examine its supporting assumptions or axioms, and therefore the value of its conclusions is a *dependent* value, directly proportionate to the value of its underlying hypotheses—and which it is in no position to assess because it does not examine its assumptions or underlying hypotheses.

It is only noetic reasoning or the forth level of understanding that assesses conclusions because it assesses the assumptions from which conclusions are deduced. Fourth-level knowing quite literally "turns everything upside down" because it recognizes the hypothetical character of the plethora of "truths" in which we find ourselves immersed, not one of which is grounded in intuition of a "first principle free from assumption" (510b).

As Plato makes eminently clear in the ensuing discussion with Glaucon, Geometry and Arithmetic, and indeed the whole of what passes for Empirical and Social Sciences among us today, belong to third-level, dianoetic knowing. But this is to say that the whole of "culture" and "science" is conditioned and dependent thinking wherein, ultimately, we know not whereof we speak.

It is only fourth-level, critical assessment of axioms and assumptions, the "exercise of reason", and which Plato will shortly refer to as *dialectics* (511c and 532a), which properly speaking deserves the designation "thinking" and "science". *But this is more because it struggles towards intuition of the unconditioned, rather than because it actually enjoys it.* Let us never forget that Socrates *doesn't know,* and that these allegories are offered by Socrates as metaphors and analogies because the force of his ascending momentum is too weak to carry him over the top.

Glaucon nicely summarizes this second allegory, clearly stating that the "arts" and "sciences" belong to the realm of *conditioned* and *dependent* thinking, and that reasoning or dialectics gives "a *clearer perception* of real being and the world of mind ..." (511c, Italics added).

The allegory of the Line, along with the later discussion of dialectics in Book VII, constitutes a more complete working out of hypothetical *logos* than we were offered in the *Meno* and in the "second voyage in search of the cause" in the *Phaedo*. And it is interesting to note that Plato uses "hypothesis" in two quite different senses: on the one hand, third-level thinking and understanding is hypothetical because it draws conclusions from unexamined assumptions; on the other hand, fourth-level thinking and reasoning is hypothetical *in the literal sense*—

> treating assumptions not as beginnings, but as literally hypotheses, that is to say steps and springboards for assault, from which it may

> push its way up to the region free of assumptions 511b

Might I call these, respectively, "*descensional* hypothetical thinking" and "*ascensional* hypothetical thinking?" Regardless, human beings are caught forever in the grips of hypothetical-*logos*.

THE ALLEGORY OF THE CAVE

The Cave is perhaps the most famous of Plato's allegories and images. It is probably no exaggeration to say that it has been the dominant operative metaphor in Western education and culture. It would indeed be an exaggeration, however, to claim that it has been interpreted uniformly these past two-thousand-odd years.

The allegory is too familiar to bear quoting here. Two points, however, must be emphasized. One, the "parable of education and ignorance" symbolizes that state of human *nature*. It is not culturally-bound to fourth century B.C. Hellas. It offers itself, rather, as a trans-cultural, 'eternal' depiction of the state of human existing. It purports, then, to be an *essential* allegory of human life. Two, the allegory is again more epistemological than ontological. It purports to describe the dynamics involved in understanding and reasoning, rather than the ontological-entitative structure of reality.

Of course at the same time it is an image of Socrates' pedagogic behavior, at least to the extent that the would-be liberator is executed by those whom he would lead out of the cave of darkness and ignorance into the world of light and knowledge. But I wouldn't try to make too much of this aspect at least in terms of a too-literal reading of the allegory, for the Cave is entirely too un-erotic to depict the behavior and impact of Socrates in any simplistic fashion.

The Cave then images the state of human beings with respect to knowledge and ignorance. And what it states quite clearly is that each and every human being is born into a given cultural situation which can be likened to an underground sight-theater, wherein citizens survey and assimilate the "sights" and the "truths" endorsed by their culture and society.

The cave is an emphatically relativistic depiction of human culture. It recognizes that various cultures view the human situation variously, and each pronounces its view *real*. Each community of cave-dwellers solemnly pronounces that its cave is *above*-ground.

Earlier I made reference to mountain climbing. Plato's cave is really a mountain climbing metaphor—remember the mist-filled hollows in the Myth of the Variegated Earth at the end of the *Phaedo*?—wherein one or a few extricate themselves from the complacency characterizing their fellow valley-dwellers, climb the surrounding mountains and see the human situation quite differently according to the varying elevations they attain. And as they skip from mountain to mountain they look down onto valley-dwellers who resolutely (and violently) insist that their valley is the whole of the human world, and that the limits of their valley-bounded vision are the limits of human vision.

The cave is an allegory of the smashing of the limits imposed on human vision. It is an image of the breaking of the bonds of human culture.

> Then we must apply this image, my dear Glaucon ... to all we have been saying. The world of our sight is like the habitation in prison, the firelight there to the sunlight here, the ascent and the view of the upper world is the rising of the soul into the world of mind; *put it so and you will not be far from my own surmise ... but God knows if it is really true.* 517 a-b (Italics added)

The Cave is a graphic depiction of the method of knowing adumbrated in the allegory of the Line. Again, it is a formal rather than a substantial depiction, and although it aspires to universal and essential reference, by no stretch of the imagination does it claim apodictic or infallible status. It is an *image* of human liberation and of movement towards maturation. Nothing more. Nothing less. Correlating the Cave with the Line we usually get something like this: life in the cave corresponds to the lower two levels of the line, the realm of sensation; life above ground corresponds to the higher two levels of the line, the realm of mind or thinking. But this is entirely too simplistic, and we must recognize that the majority of peoples do not push their way into fourth-level thinking or dialectics, but are content with third-level understanding. The real dividing line, *the* significant division in the allegory of the Line that correlates with emergence from the Cave, lies between levels three and four, between understanding and reasoning.

Even accepting this line of demarcation as especially relevant, thinking as such (i.e., the *two* levels of thinking) is a far cry from the grovelling complacency of sensation—for sensation or sensibility does seem to have an air of complacency and *stasis* about it for Plato, and it is for this reason, it seems to me, that he insists on the supra-sensibility of reasoning or dialectics. But thinking, to retrieve now its two levels, can be unquestioning or questioning with respect to its own grounding.

The realm of mind or thinking, therefore, must be subdivided, with Plato, into understanding and reasoning. But let me pick up on Plato with the continuation of the above quotation:

> At least, what appears to me is, that in the world of the known, *last of all, is the idea of the good, and with what toil to be seen!* And seen, this must be inferred to be the cause of all right and beautiful things for all, which gives birth to light and the king of light in the world of sight, and, in the world of mind, herself the queen produces truth and reason; and she must be seen by one who is to act with reason publicly or privately. 517 b-c (Italics added)

Here we have a parting of the ways in interpreting Plato. Does the liberated prisoner intuit the good, or not? I have emphasized selected words and phrases because therein I detect a hesitancy and a guessing that is quite removed from intuition and infallible proclamation. And, of course, to claim the latter would be to deny the image of human excellence instantiated in Socrates who knew that he did not know.

Two points remain to be considered. The first might be called a motivational factor and is at best only hinted-at by Plato. I refer to the role of *light* in the allegory of the Cave. In one respect, we might see Plato here tying in the allegory of the Sun, or even perhaps the seductiveness of the Beautiful from the *Symposium*. Regardless, I suggest that it is the presence of *light* in the depths of the Cave which not only, obviously, produces the shadows and images attended to, but also attracts and motivates the prisoner to enquire and question and eventually extricate her/himself from cultural bondage.

What Plato intimates is that the majority of people fixate on shadows and never do see or respond to the light. But what this in turn implies is that to be a human being, prisoner or not, is to be open to the light, for fixation on shadows presupposes openness to light, without which there are no shadows!

To be fully alive, of course, is to respond to the promptings of the light by ascending the Line and extricating ourselves from the Cave.

The second is the educational factor:

> Then if this is true ... our belief about these matters must be this, that the nature of education is not really such as some of its professors say it is; as you know, they say that there is not understanding in the soul, but they put it in, as if they were putting sight into blind eyes ... .

> But our reasoning indicates ... that this power is already in the soul of each, and is the instrument by which each learns; thus if the eye could not see without being turned with the whole body from the dark towards the light, so this instrument must be turned round with the whole soul away from the world of becoming until it is able to endure the sight of being and the most brilliant light of being ... 518 b-c

Education and its concomitant liberation is not simply the assimilation of facts and information. Education is *thinking;* it is questioning and probing, critically assessing the cultural convictions within which we find ourselves. Metaphorically, education is the turning away from shadows to the light, and following this light out of the cave into the brightness of day wherein we can view the realities above ground and, ultimately, intuit the sun itself. In fine, education is the actualization of the responsiveness-to-light that constitutes us as human beings in the first place.

Socrates terminates the discussion of the allegories with the memorable:

> the turning of a soul round from a day which is like night to a true day—this is the ascent into real being, which we shall say is true philosophy. 521 c

and then proceeds to discuss in some detail the dynamics of the studies which will liberate human beings and lead them into philosophy and human excellence.

The discussion focuses on ambiguity, specifically the ambiguity of relative qualities which propels us to seek thoughtful resolution and clarification. The theme is initiated through a discussion of the material and organizational value that the study of mathematics has for students of leadership. It quickly settles upon the resolutoryclarificatory power of *calculation* when confronted with qualitative ambiguity.

> I mean by those which do not invite thought ... all those which do not pass from one sensation to its opposites at the same time. Those that do, when the sensation shows two opposites equally .... 523 b-c,

and again,

> I distinguish as provocative of thought those which bring their opposites with them when they fall upon the senses, and, as not awaking the intelligence, all such as do not bring in their opposites. 524d

Socrates now leads Glaucon through an agenda of studies proceeding from arithmetic through geometry (plane and solid) to astronomy and harmonics in which each, in a progressively hierarchical manner, thoughtfully clarifies and resolves the ambiguities of its subordinate subject-matter. And these hierarchically integrated arts and sciences themselves point towards the one science of *dialectics* (531d) :

> Then, my dear Glaucon ... is this the law at last, which dialectic brings out to its final meaning, and which being the *law of mind* would have a likeness in the *power of sight* trying, as we described it, to look at last upon living things themselves, and the sun itself? Just so when a man tries by discussion to get a start towards the real thing, through reason and without any help from the senses, and will not desist until he grasps by thought alone the real nature of good itself, he arrives at the very end of the world of thought, as the other before was at the end of the world of sight. 532a-b

And now Socrates proceeds to integrate the three allegories, claiming that the study of the arts and the sciences are but *preparatory studies,* for, although they stir up and bring out the best in the soul (532c), and liberate the prisoner from the darkness and ignorance of the cave, for all that they leave her/him in *dreamland* (533c) *because they do not examine the hypotheses upon which they are built.*

Again Socrates warns Glaucon of the supra-human task confronting them, and in effect relegates the whole of the clarification procedure they are pursuing to hypothesizing and fallibilistic guessing:

> You will not be able ... to follow me further, my dear Glaucon, although on my part there would be no want of good will. I should be glad to show you, if I could, no longer an image of what we speak of, but the truth as it appears to me, at least—*although whether really so or not, I dare not say for certain;* but I must certainly say that what we should see is something like that. 533a (Italics added)

Socrates then proceeds to elaborate once again the fourth level of the Line, emphasizing this time the questioning of hypotheses in the pursuit of a suppositionless, supra-hypothetical beginning.

The educational program outlined focuses on the progressive clarification and integration of the world of human experience in terms of hierarchically-grounded hypotheses/suppositions. And while the program strives towards a supra-hypothetical, suppositionless intuition which will absolutely clarify and integrate the whole, it is emphasized that infallibility and absolute knowledge remains forever beyond our reach.

CONCLUSION

The three allegories from the central part of the *Republic* graphically articulate Plato's anthropology and epistemology.

Human beings, for Plato, are primarily *logical* animals. That is to say, we are thinking animals, and the goal of human thinking is nothing short of *thinking the whole of reality*.

We *desire* to *understand* the whole. We *are* this desire, in fact.

But comprehensive understanding and apodictic certitude lie beyond our reach, forever beyond our reach. What does lie within our reach, however, and with which we continually find ourselves occupied, is the formation of clarifying and integrating interpretations of the whole. But each interpretation is built upon sets of assumptions which must be uncovered and tested, if we are ever to actualize this desire to understand the whole.

To the degree that interpretations are built upon suppositions or hypotheses, and successively higher (or deeper) interpretations are built upon successively higher (or deeper) suppositions, the intellectually-erotic thrust that we are is forever doomed to frustration.

In the words of Jean-Paul Sartre, then, we can say that for Plato human nature is a "useless passion!" *But what a Passion!!*

INTERPRETATION

Once upon a time in my youth, I cherished like many another the hope of entering upon a political career as soon as I came of age. It fell out, moreover, that political events took the following course. There were many who heaped abuse on the form of government then prevailing and a revolution occurred. In this revolution ... thirty came into power as supreme rulers of the whole state. Some of these happened to be relatives and acquaintances of mine, who accordingly invited me forthwith to join them, assuming my fitness for the task. No wonder that, young as I was, I cherished the belief that they would lead the city from an unjust life, as it were, to habits of justice and "manage it", as they put it, so that I was intensely interested to see what would come of it.

Of course I saw in a short time that these men made the former government look in comparison like an age of gold. Among other things, they sent an elderly man, Socrates, a friend of mine, who I should hardly be ashamed to say was the justest man of his time, in company with others, against one of the citizens to fetch him forcibly to be executed. Their purpose was to connect Socrates with their government, whether he wished or not. He refused and risked any consequences rather than become their partner in wicked deeds. When I observed all this—and some other similar matters of importance—I withdrew in disgust from the abuses of those days. Not long after came the fall of the Thirty and of their whole system of government.

Once more, less hastily this time, but surely, I was moved by the desire to take part in public life and in politics... As it chanced, however, some of those in control brought against this associate of mine, Socrates, whom I have mentioned, a most sacrilegious charge, which he least of all men deserved. They put him on trial for impiety and the people condemned and put to death the man who had refused to take part in the wicked arrest of one of their friends...

Now as I considered these matters, as well as the sort of men who were active in politics, and the laws and the customs, the more I examined them and the more I advanced in years, the harder it appeared to me to administer the government correctly... The result was that I, who had at first been full of eagerness for a public career, as I gazed upon the whirlpool of public life and saw the incessant movement of shifting currents, at last felt dizzy ... Hence I was forced to say in praise of the correct philosophy that it affords a vantage point from which we can discern in all cases what is just for communities and for individuals, and that accordingly the human race will not see better days until either the stock of those who rightly and genuinely follow philosophy acquire political authority, or else the class who have political control be led by some dispensation of

> providence to become real philosophers.
> *Letter VII* 324b-326b[1]

There are many different ways to approach the philosophy of Plato, and one of the best, I think, is suggested by the author of the *Seventh Letter*—whether it is Plato himself or not is irrelevant. Plato is a *political* thinker. But more than just this, he is a *radical* and *revolutionary* political thinker *who wants to fabricate and substitute a wholly different brand of politics for the kind then prevailing.*

And we must not ignore the role played by the historical Socrates in this project. Socrates seems to have impacted on Plato in the manner of what can only be called a "religious conversion." Socrates, the *just* man, turned Plato from the injustices of the prevailing politics to a life-long pursuit of *just* politics.

But this is misleading, for our English "politics" has a much narrower connotation than *"Politike"* had for Plato. *"Politike"* can best be translated, perhaps, as "culture", as a comprehensive culture that at once describes the whole of the human situation and, at the same time, focuses on human excellence, how we can best live our human life. Such "culture", then, encompasses what we have parcelled out to the natural and social sciences, to the fine arts, to philosophy and religion, as well to "politics" in the narrow sense of the term. It has a decidedly "existential" flavor to it.

What the author of the *Seventh Letter* tells us, simply, is that "culture" has broken down, and that until an appropriately human culture, an appropriate image and pattern of human excellence is constructed, the human race will find no peace.

The discovery and development of this new and appropriate image of human excellence is precisely the goal that Plato sets for

---

1 *The Collected Dialogues of Plato, op. cit..*

himself. He found it first adumbrated in the living Socrates, and he presents it to us in his dialogues incorporated in the person and behavior of his literary Socrates.

Do we find it there? Do the dialogues burn our ears with their iconoclastic and revolutionary message? At least the contemporaries of the living Socrates reacted to his message—they killed him for it! But do we even hear it?

I think it is imperative that we do hear it today and tomorrow—yes, especially tomorrow, for we are entering an era when for the first time we will *be able to hear* it, and it just might shake us up the way old Socrates shook up Plato.

But I do not want this to be yet another "historical" study. The human mind is a historical vagabond, a wide-ranging surveyor of deeds and possibilities whenever and wherever they are found. Any instant of history can be made contemporary with any other instant—at least abstractly. Nevertheless, various problematics and possibilities sometimes reoccur in the course of history when particular circumstances are especially relevant to the appearance of these problematics and these possibilities. Such would seem to be our situation today, and I will try to demonstrate in the course of this Interpretation that Socrates can be a significant contemporary of ours, and might very well be a crucially necessary contemporary if we are to thrive in this late twentieth, early-twenty-first-century A.D. era of ours.

But I'm running ahead of myself.

Yes, Plato first glimpsed the *new man,* the new image and model of human excellence, in the person and behavior of his elder friend, Socrates, and he incorporated and developed it in the character of Socrates in his dialogues. And no, Western Culture is not footnoted to Plato, as innumerable teachers of philosophy have drummed into their students' heads. *Western culture is anti-Plato,* regardless of professorial protestations to the contrary.

So what about this Western Culture? What about the appropriateness and viability of the current image of human excellence that prevails in this late twentieth-century Western world of ours?

The Western world, comprising about one-third of the human population of Earth, is doing rather well, thank you very much. But, a growing number of voices admonish us, it is is doing well for itself by exploiting the remaining two thirds of humanity! And how well are we, the "developed" and industrialized world, faring with the environment, and with the cleanliness of our air and water? Is the "green house" effect really taking hold, and is the protective layer of ozone really being dissipated? And do we care? Ah! the Bomb, and ICBM's—annoying little nuisances, aren't they?

The point about all of this is that each and every factor in the various crises affecting twentieth-century humanity is a product and issue of human culture. None of them has been visited upon us from afar. They are home-grown, the proud achievements of proud traditions. And the Western technological, nuclear tradition is leading the lot!

The only sensible conclusion that we can draw from this is that Western Culture has broken down. It has self-destructed, or at least is well on the way towards self-destruction. The very success of our industrialized and technologized culture today proclaims its long-term *un*viability, and demonstrates that the inner structure and logic of Western Culture has been askew for some time, some centuries even. We desperately need a new image and model of human excellence. We desperately need a new "politics" and a new "culture".

Enter Socrates.

And enter Socrates for two reasons: One, the Socrates who is the progenitor and godfather of many of our problems, and must now be exorcised. Two, the "real" Socrates, the Socrates never emulated by our tradition and who stands as a challenge to this tradition—the Socrates who might "save" us, even as he might have saved, but did not, Athens and the Hellenic world.

So there you have it—you thought you had caught me contradicting myself, and here I've gone and revealed the cards hidden in my hand! Yes, Western Culture is indeed footnoted to Socrates and Plato, but to a *pseudo* Socrates and to a *pseudo* Plato that is diametrically opposed to the *real* Socrates and the *real* Plato whom, as I mentioned above, we are perhaps today in a position to hear for the very first time.

Alfred North Whitehead somewhere says that Western philosophy is a series of footnotes to Plato. For our purposes, we can understand philosophy as being synonymous with culture, and the verdict of history would seem to be that Whitehead is correct. Our Western culture is an industrialized-*Platonic*-culture, and the designation "Judeo-Christian" is really quite wide of the mark.

"Platonic" culture summons forth images of dichotomies: Soul vs. Body, Spirit vs. Matter, Being vs. Becoming and Intelligibility vs. Sensibility. Platonism is *dualistic,* and teaches quite plainly that humanity's home is in the World of Ideas, in the Intelligible Heaven from which we were cast out to sojourn for a time in the dross of this material and sensible world. Our ideational and ideological response to this exile is to control and manipulate matter and sensibility. Our *Platonic* response to this exile is, and necessarily must needs be, the development of bureaucracy.

The Platonic theory of knowledge underscores this dualism, for it states that understanding and discovery are but *remembering* what we saw in "heaven" and which, amidst the distractions of sensation, we have forgotten.

Beneath it all is the fervent belief that we *can remember* and we *can know.* Philosophy is king, and under its direction peace can be offered to us, and we can escape the pains of sensible life and return to the World of Ideas where we shall be happy forever.

Granted, this is somewhat of a "Christianized" version of the Platonic legacy, but it is what has fuelled our Western Culture on and off for some two thousand years. (Remember that Nietzsche called Christianity "Platonism for the masses.") And what it has taught us, and what we have eagerly learned is twofold: *absolute knowledge can be ours,* and this *absolute knowledge can control and direct our lives.* Knowledge can be ours, and knowledge is power. The rest, as we say, is history.

For centuries the West struggled with the collapse of the Ancient World, and contented itself with mysticized and imagistic versions of Platonism. It probably could have done little else. Then the long collecting and gathering era that we refer to as the Middle Ages exploded in the profusion of knowledge that ushered in the Modern age. The Industrial Revolution and the Electric and Atomic ages followed in rapid succession. Indeed, knowledge *is* ours, and knowledge *is* power!

But lately this power seems to be running amok and feeding on itself to the extent that the long-term survival of the human race is in jeopardy. Something has gone wrong, and we had better set about rectifying it pretty quickly.

Our cultural success has thrived on the two proclamations of knowledge and power. The second is really an appendage to the first, and it is the arrogance of the first, the arrogance of this claim to knowledge, which more than anything characterizes our Western Culture.

And this culture is a footnote to Plato. But is it really? How easily we forget that Plato taught that Socrates' claim to fame, his one claim to human excellence, was his recognition that he knew that *he knew nothing,* he knew that *he did not know.* Pray tell, how can we ground knowing in *not*-knowing, science in *ne*science?

Before I parade Socrates on stage, let me address two objections that might trip us up at this point in our enquiry. One. How is it possible for Socrates to *know* that he does *not know*? Is this not a contradiction? If the knowing and the not-knowing occurred on the same level and were directed at the same "object", yes it would be a contradiction. But for Socrates they occur on different levels and intend different "objects", so there is no contradiction. Socrates and Plato interpret knowing as a revelatory activity. First level or primary knowledge (and these designations are mine, not Plato's) reveals the objective other, the world. Second level or secondary and reflective knowledge reveals the knower (the subject) engaged in first-level, object-revealing-activity. Socrates' statement that he knows (subjectively) that he does not know (objectively) bespeaks a degree of self-awareness that is quite removed from self-contradiction and from objective infallibility. Two. I do not consider Socratic philosophizing any sort of panacea. I do not consider Socrates any sort of *savior*. No. Socrates is an "idea". He is a sign pointing towards an attitude and a mode of behavior which *might* very well .... But I'll pick this up later on in my concluding remarks.

The "real" Socrates, then. Now quite obviously, I'm not going to talk about the real flesh and blood Socrates who has been dead these past two thousand plus years. I've never met the man. Nor am I going to talk about the real Socrates of the Platonic dialogues, in any sense of the definitive interpretation of the Socrates that Plato presents us in his dialogues. Plato, I suppose, could give us this, but he's been dead for two thousand plus years, too. No, neither of these.

The "real" Socrates that I will talk about is "Cronin's Socrates", Socrates such as I interpret him through my readings of the dialogues. But I hope not through my own private, idiosyncratic reading. I hope that my reading can interact with your reading so that together we might interact with this well-spring of our cultural tradition.

Socrates lived, largely, throughout the period of Athenian glory. He was born in the third decade after the battles of Marathon and Salamis wherein Athens gained a decisive victory for "democracy" over Persian tyranny. He witnessed the rise of Athenian naval power, and the establishment of the Athenian "empire". He lived throughout the age of Pericles, and witnessed the completion of the Parthenon and the flourishing of the Arts. Finally, he fought in the Peloponnesian wars and observed the defeat of Athens by Sparta.

The rise and fall of Athens, outwardly told, is a sad chronicle of human events. Sadder by far, however, is the inward story, the *moral rise* of Athens in her noble defense of freedom against slavery, and the *moral fall* of Athens as evidenced in her proclamation (*via* Thucydides) to the Melian peoples that "might is right". Well might Socrates have pondered the collapse of culture and the breakdown of tradition!

And he was not alone in such pondering. Athens was flooded with hawkers and peddlers of science and sophistry, religion and *realpolitik*. Confusion abounded, and Athens rode the crest of the wave of pride and expansionism that knew no discipline or restraint—until it came crashing down in 403 BC, and until it crashed even further for Plato when in 399 BC the revived democracy executed Socrates, "the justest man of his time".

Now Plato was well aware of two absolute necessities of human life: one, we need "culture", and two, arising out of this need, we *fabricate* a culture.

Such "culture" is nothing technical. It is simply the "view of the world" in which a society wraps itself. It is the prevailing pattern of behavior circumscribing relations between persons and between persons and the gods. It is the reigning model of human excellence by which, individually and collectively, men and women direct themselves in the course of their daily lives.

The value of "culture" lies in its *viability*, in its ability continuingly to direct and develop the human lives encompassed by it. And it was precisely the viability of the Athenian and Hellenic culture which died in the debacle that was the Peloponnesian wars and the execution of Socrates. Hellenic culture had produced a proud and aggressive Athens that felt justified in exploiting her smaller and weaker neighbors, until her greed precipitated a military engagement with Sparta which ended in her defeat. Injustice abounded, and Athens and the whole of Hellenic culture proved themselves to be morally corrupt. The only recourse was to erect a new culture, a new model and pattern of justice and human excellence.

Plato accepted the challenge, and in his dialogues he set about to erect this new culture, this new model and pattern of justice and human excellence. It seems incontestable that he first glimpsed this new culture in the person and behavior of the living Socrates. Subsequently, he set about to develop and elaborate it, and presented it to the world incarnated in the person and behavior of his literary Socrates.

The constant focus of the literary Socrates is on *logos* and on logical behavior. But what is *logos*? What does it mean to say that "man is a *logical* animal"? And how do we behave *logically* anyway?

The force of Socrates' question is perhaps lost on us today because of the prevailing assumption that we all know what "logical" means. But try this out for a minute. The basic meaning of the Greek "*Logos*" is "speech" or "word". Let us say, "talk". Socrates, as it were, barged into a room full of people talking their heads off and shouted at them—talk! talk! Talk? But we are talking! What do you mean? Are you crazy?

Crazy? Perhaps. But what if for all the 'talking' going on in the room, there is very little *real* talking going on? Do we know how to talk? And what does it mean to "talk" anyway?

Logos was transcribed by the Romans as *ratio,* which became our English "rational". And so Socrates' question now becomes, What is "rational" and "reasonable"? And how must we behave if we are to behave rationally or reasonably?

We are not born ready-made rational animals. Of this Plato was certain. We must become rational. But to do so, we must first have some indication of what constitutes *logos,* of what constitutes reasonableness and rationality.

It is almost as if Plato is saying to succeeding generations: look, I first caught a glimpse of rationality in Socrates. But Socrates is dead. Here then is a literary Socrates in whom you, too, might catch a glimpse of rationality, through whom you, too, might discover the meaning of human life.

In the so-called "early" and "middle" dialogues Plato presents Socrates quite concretely, and engaged in lively discussion with the then contemporary peddlers of culture and of rationality. Socrates talks with Poets, Soldiers, Priests and Sophists. He discourses on natural science, morality, religion and rhetoric. And throughout it all he consistently focuses on *logos,* justice and goodness. He consistently deprecates and opposes the traditional and the then contending models of human excellence, and challenges his interlocutors and readers to join with him in a search for a new model of excellence.

The simplest matters are often the most difficult to discover. And for all the noise we have produced concerning the difficulty and the complexity of Platonic philosophy, Socrates' message in these early and middle dialogues is really very simple. It is that *we do not know* that knowledge lies forever beyond the reach of human beings.

Is that simple enough for you? Yes, and absolutely shattering for those in Socrates' day who demanded the security of knowledge and who needed to know that they knew and to know that they were right. And not only in Socrates' day!—"my country, right or wrong!" and "I belong to the true Church!" Political dogmatism and fanaticism still abound.

> Then supposing you should ever hence-forth try to conceive afresh, Theaetetus, if you succeed, your embryo thoughts will be better as a consequence of today's scrutiny, and if you remain barren, you will be gentler and more agreeable to your companions, having the good sense not to fancy you know what you do not know. For that, and no more, is all that my art can effect; nor have I any of that knowledge possessed by all the great and admirable men of our own day or of the past.
> *Theaetetus* 210b-c[1]

Whatever Theaetetus' reaction to the recognition of his own not-knowing might have been, gentleness and agreeableness decidedly are not the widespread reaction today. But what if Socrates is right? What if we do not know, and if our pretensions to knowing are precisely that, pretensions? And what if whatever claim to knowledge we might legitimately make is grounded in and nourished by this very not-knowing itself?

Plato, anyway, was convinced that such indeed was the human condition, and in the early dialogues he presented Socrates in conversation with then contemporary pretenders-to-knowledge. Socrates undermines and ridicules their pretension. And in the middle dialogues he continues the attack, but now supplements it with

---

1 *Ibidem.*

a positive assessment of human knowledge and a positive development of our capacity to know.

In many ways, Sophistry is the great challenge that Socrates faced throughout his life. The Sophists were an itinerant group of teachers and scholars who contributed to the spread of the emerging "natural sciences" and significantly to the development of Elocution and Grammar. But they were also self-conscious "how-to-succeeders", cultural relativists, opportunists, and pretenders-to-knowledge. Socrates did not like the Sophists, and Western Culture quite uncritically has adopted his attitude, and has thereby failed to detect in Sophistry what Socrates so clearly saw and feared.

The central message of Sophistry is that human beings fashion their own culture. We fashion our gods and our truths, our morality and our politics. Truth is fiction and, in the words of perhaps the greatest of the Sophists, Protagoras, "Man is the measure of all that is."

Now Socrates buys this! *Socrates is a Sophist,* at least to the extent that he recognizes that we fashion our own culture, that we fashion truth, and that truth, therefore, is fiction! Yes, man is indeed the measure of all that is.

But, unlike Protagoras and his fellow Sophists, Socrates does not stop here. For while it might very well be the case that "man is the measure of all that is", Socrates proclaims that *Logos is the measure of man; Logos is the measure of human reality!*

What, then, is *Logos*? And, along with this and even more important perhaps, what are we such that we seek and are measured by *Logos*?

Throughout the early dialogues Plato demonstrates that preceding and prevailing Hellenic culture did *not* seek *Logos*, and was decidedly anti-*logos* or illogical. Consistently Plato demonstrates that Socrates' interlocutors, the purveyors of traditional and the then contemporary culture, did *not* understand what they said, and inconsistently and even contradictorily related ideas to ideas and ideas to practice. Positively, these early dialogues are inconclusive. But negatively, as it were, we can see emerging therein the criteria of clarity, consistency and integrity as characteristic of the "new image of human excellence" and the "new culture".

It is in the middle dialogues that Plato undertakes the positive development and elucidation of this "new image and pattern of human excellence" and "new culture" so demanded by the political disruptions of his day. The *Apology*, the *Meno*, the *Phaedo*, the *Symposium* and the *Republic* present a surprisingly detailed and systematically developed new cultural paradigm, a *new image of human excellence.*

Whatever the order of composition, and the five listed are by no means exhaustive of the middle-period positive development, Plato in effect launches his project with the *Apology*. Therein he specifies his opposition, and lays down the touch-stone of the 'new model of human excellence', the reality of human not-knowing, the recognition "that human wisdom is worth little or nothing" (23a).

Much of the *Apology* is given over to the task of deflating Poetry as *the* channel of culture.

Poetry cut a much wider swath then than it does today, and in attacking the pretension-to-knowledge of Homeric poetry, Plato was attacking the very heart of the Athenian and Hellenic cultural tradition.

But one does not easily turn one's back on one's cultural tradition, wipe the slate clean as it were, and start all over again. Cultural progression occurs by way of discontinuity insinuating itself within continuity, and so Plato presents Socrates and Socratic philosophy as the *new* Homeric hero, the *new* poetic Demigod who exemplifies and incarnates the new values of human excellence, the new value of "enquiry" and "examination of one's soul".

Philosophy supplants Poetry as the purveyor of human excellence. And Socrates is the paradigmatic philosopher, Socrates who knew that he did not know and, on the basis of this recognition, was deemed by Apollo to be the wisest person in Hellas.

Apart from admonishing us to attend to our own not-knowing, to examine and test ourselves and to care for goodness and truth, the *Apology,* tells us precious little about the "soul" we are to examine, very little about how we are to think, and little about the goodness and truth for which we are to care. These very *lacunae* indicate the program of enquiry that Plato pursues in the succeeding middle dialogues.

The *Meno* is connected dramatically to the *Apology* through Anytos who makes a cameo appearance in the former, and is of course one of the accusers of Socrates in the latter. His role in the *Meno* is not simply to effect a formal connection between these two dialogues, but rather to underscore, negatively and by contradiction, the central message of the *Meno* itself. This message is the delineation of the logic or structure of hypothetical reasoning. It is, simply, the delineation of *Hypothetical Logos.*

The *Apology* left us with the question, How does one do philosophy? How does one think as Socrates thinks? The *Meno* gives us a preliminary response, a preliminarily formal response and a concrete demonstration of the actual hypothetical thinkingof Socrates.

The *Meno* can be divided into four parts. Part one delineates the structure of *definitional logic* or addresses the question of how one properly forms definitions. Part two delineates the structure of *hypothetical logic* or addresses the question of how one engages in rational enquiry. This structure is explained mythically, and contextually exemplified in the discovery of the Pythagorean Theorem in the discussion with the slave-boy. Part three, using the hypothetical logic already delineated, investigates the question that, purportedly, is the focus of the dialogue, and concludes that virtue probably is not teachable. Part four differentiates knowledge and right or true opinion.

Part one is simple and straightforward, but it does entail some unnerving consequences. Socrates insists that definitions are statements of essence, of essential whatness, and are to be composed of ingredients that are simple, independently known and agreed to. But this is to claim that definitions bespeak an infallible knowledge of whatever it is the definition purports to define. And it is to claim that definitions entail absolute knowledge of the constituents of definitions.

The *not*-knowing Socrates of the *Apology* quite obviously is excluded from trafficking in such "definitions". But not so Menon the Rhetor who has often delivered fine speeches, so he claims, on the definition of virtue. However, when pressed by Socrates to define virtue according to the canons of definition laid down, Menon is reduced to dumbness.

None of this surprises us, and Plato is after all only setting the stage for the delivery of the message of the *Meno* which immediately follows.

Menon introduces the matter of hypothetical logic by challenging the very possibility of enquiry as search: how can one look for what one does not already know? and how could one ever conclude one's search without already knowing what it is for which one is searching?

It is important to appreciate that Menon's challenge is a *direct assault* upon the image of human excellence which Socrates adumbrated in the *Apology*! This is no simply dramatic tiff between Socrates and Menon. *It is rather a direct challenge to Socratic-enquiry as being any paradigm whatsoever of human excellence.*

Socrates, you remember, claims that he does not know, and that on the basis of the conscious appropriation of his not-knowing he is open to enquiry and search. Indeed, human excellence consists in just this enquiring-after and searching-for what we do not know, and to which Menon replies—Nonsense! Not-knowing numbs us and relegates us to immobility. Knowledge and knowledge alone confers upon as the crown of excellence.

And so the combatants are distinguished: the person of not-knowing-wanting-to-know vs. the person of knowledge; the Hypothesist vs. the Dogmatist.

Socrates responds to Menon's challenge by telling the tale told by priests and priestesses that the soul has migrated through many lives, and so learning and enquiry in any one life is simply remembering what befell it in a former life. He even characterizes this tale as a *reasoned explanation* by the priests and priestesses in question!

Now if you fail to see the *irony* in this—as, indeed, our cultural tradition has by and large failed to see it!--then there is nothing I can do. I most certainly cannot force you to see it, any more than Plato could.

Having delivered himself of this "mythical justification", Socrates proceeds to demonstrate in action the actuality of enquiry and search in his discussion with the slave-boy. He doesn't waste any time trying to convince Menon of the possibility of enquiry. He demonstrates its actuality in action!

Ostensibly demonstrating the truth of the "reasoned explanation" of the priests and priestesses, the exchange with the slave-boy is actually a concrete demonstration of enquiry in action utilizing the *hypothetical and experimental method of reasoning*. Look at what happens: the boy guesses or hypothesizes what the sought-after answer is. Socrates draws the hypothesized figure in the sand. The boy is wrong. He tries again, that is to say, he offers a new guess or hypothesis. This is tested, and it fails. He tries again, and so on. Far from being a demonstration of the truthfulness of any priestly tale of remembering or recollection, this is a demonstration of the hypothetical-empirical method that we today refer to simply as the "scientific method". *And this is its first appearance in history.*

The logic of hypothetical-empirical thinking is what the *Meno* is all about. And the message of the *Meno* is that the new pattern of thinking practiced by the 'new man', by the philosopher-Socrates, the new paradigm of human excellence, is *self-conscious hypothetical thinking* grounded in the recognition that one does not know and wants to know.

Enter Anytos.

The role assigned to Anytos in this dialogue seems to be to underscore the new model of human excellence exemplified in the person and behavior of Socrates. As well as reminding us of the *Apology,* Anytos emphasizes the fact that, willy-nilly, *human beings think hypothetically,* and that the challenge facing them is to do so self-consciously and self-reflectively. Seen against the back-drop of what has occurred in the *Meno* before his appearance, Anytos manifestly thinks hypothetically. But he does not know it. He is not aware of it. And his very not-knowing, i.e., his not-knowing that he does-not-know, in contrast to the self-conscious not-knowing of Socrates and the slave-boy, catapults him into dogmatism.

So we return to the contrast between the hypothesist and the dogmatist, and Plato seems to be telling us that human thinking is inevitably hypothetical, but not inevitably or even usually consciously so. And when thinking is not pursued self-consciously-hypothetically it easily degenerates into the blinded dogmatism of an Anytos and his fellow Athenians who visited injustice upon Socrates.

One of the more important dimensions of hypothetical thinking developed in the *Meno* is the empirical (or experiential) testing that Socrates utilizes in his discussion with the slave-boy, and then emphasizes in his subsequent discussion with Menon. Socrates and Menon were discussing the teachability of virtue on the assumption that virtue was knowledge, or at least related in some way to knowledge. But the empirical evidence that no such teaching had ever occurred, or, perhaps better, the absence of any empirical evidence that such teaching had ever occurred, prompted them to reassess the original assumption or hypothesis. Now this reassessment is important, and it indicates two things: One, hypothetical thinking is about the empirical world, and must needs be tested in the empirical world. Two, hypothetical thinking is inevitably fallible.

Unfortunately—but I will argue shortly that this judgment must be qualified rather severely—empirical testing does not receive much development or emphasis in subsequent dialogues. It is there, but it is easily overlooked. And it has been overlooked, thereby contributing to the failure of our tradition to appreciate the central focus on the logic of experimental-hypothetical thinking in the *Meno* and subsequent dialogues.

And what are the implications of such fallibilistic, hypothetical thinking? Perhaps Plato touches on some of these when he concludes the *Meno* by having Socrates insist that opinion might be no worse a guide for action than knowledge. Of course he speaks of right or true opinion, and we are left dangling as to how, confined to opinions and hypotheses as we seem to be, we could ever definitively designate any opinion as right or true.

Plato is certainly conscious of the problematic situation in which the philosopher thus finds himself. I am reminded of the remark of John Macmurray concerning Immanuel Kant that while he agreed with the romantic assessment of reason, he found it intolerable that fact was thereby reduced to fiction. Kant thought he extricated himself from the dilemma. How did Plato handle it?

> Yes, I think that I argue well, Menon. I would not be confident in everything I say about the argument; but one thing I would fight for to the end, both in word and in the deed if I were able—that if we believed that we must try to find out what is not known, we should be better and braver and less idle than if we believed that what we do not know it is impossible to find out and that we need not even try. 86 b-c

> ... if it is impossible in company with the body to know anything purely, one thing of two follows: either knowledge is possible nowhere, or only after death .... 66 e

Traditional interpretations of Plato's theory of knowledge consistently have either ignored this dichotomy or have come down on the mythical side of possessing pure knowledge "after death". This is most unfortunate and, at the same time, it is very pleasant for soft people to hear (Cf. *Meno,* 81d), for it removes us from any and all responsibility for seeking knowledge in this world before death.

Rather than any demonstration of the belief in personal immortality, and the grounding of knowledge in such immortality, I contend that the *Phaedo* demonstrates that to know anything purely is beyond our capacity (both before death *and* after death), and that herein Plato offers us a further investigation into and development of the logic of hypothetical reasoning.

In the *Phaedo,* furthermore, he pulls out all stops and in a surprisingly forthright manner he presents Philosophy, exemplified in the person and behavior of Socrates pictured in discussion with his friends on the last day of his life, as the supplanting of Mystical Religion and the whole of preceding Hellenic culture.

The *Phaedo* is one of the more complex of Plato's dialogues, and, if read properly (*I* contend), is seen to be focused singularly on the question of the viability and the value of *Logos*, of *hypothetical reasoning*, as the new pattern of human behavior constitutive of human excellence.

At first glance it might seem that the dialogue is arguing that such human excellence entails the radical and complete separation of the soul from the body, and of intellection from sensation. The first third of the dialogue indeed emphasizes just such a separation of soul from body and transcendence of intellection over sensation. But this dualism is dramatically contextualized by the mixture theme of the opening scene wherein Socrates presents himself as once again before his judges, and announces his hope that his defense of the knowing-not-knowing of Philosophy as the new model of human excellence will be more successful this second time around.

Can culturally-bound human beings easily come to grips with not-knowing? Can we rest comfortably with the realization that we do not "know anything purely"? Socrates' interlocutors in this last discussion could not, and indeed we must see their literal acceptance of the various 'proofs for immortality' offered in this dialogue as grounded in this very inability, as is their childish fear that the soul at death might be dissipated in the wind. Consistent with his ironic temperament, Socrates advises them to take care that they depart this life on a calm day!

The heart of the *Phaedo*, and the message that Plato offers us in this dialogue, is contained in Socrates' "second voyage in search of the cause". Plato takes great care to isolate this scene dramatically from the rest of the dialogue, and he presents it as a response to the direct challenge voiced both by Socrates' interlocutors and Echecrates that *Logos* was no longer trustworthy.

In the earlier arguments for immortality Cebes and Simmias had convinced themselves that they had found pure knowledge, absolute and infallible certitude. Subsequently, having been brought to doubt this conviction, like spoiled children they blame reason rather than themselves, and cry out that reason, *Logos,* cannot be trusted. They thus fall victim to Misology, *the worst disease,* Socrates claims, that can befall human beings.

Socrates' autobiographical "second voyage" is a direct response to this virulent attack by Misology, and his vanquishing of the same prompts his final charge to his friend Criton that they owe a cock to Asclepios, the god of healing.

What is of interest is *how the healing in question was effected.* What is of interest are the ministrations and medicaments applied by Socrates to effect the cure that is acknowledged both at the conclusion of the autobiographical scene and in Socrates' final command to Criton.

The answer, quite simply, is *hypothetical reasoning.* And the *Phaedo* offers us a more detailed development of hypothetical reasoning than was presented in the *Meno.*

But even this development is far from complete, for only one side or dimension of two-sided hypothesizing is developed. By two-sidedness, I refer to direction or orientation on the one hand, and method or procedure on the other. As we shall see, Socrates develops only the method or procedure in the *Phaedo.*

Hypothesizing is introduced formally by Socrates in response to the disappointment he experienced in investigating the philosophy of Anaxagoras. He had been very excited by the latter's claim that "Mind is the arranger and cause of all things" (97c), and expected that he would find in his writings *why* everything was arranged the way it was. He thought that mind would arrange everything for the best, and so he eagerly sought this "best" or "good" in Anaxagoras' writings. But his hopes were dashed, and so he embarked on his own "second voyage in search of the cause" (99c).

"One understands only when one sees things in the light of perfection."[1] One understands the action of the Athenian judges in condemning Socrates only when one envisions the "good" or "perfection" which prompted them to act as they did. One understands Socrates' abiding by their judgment only when one envisions the "good" or "perfection" which prompted him so to abide. But by no means does Anaxagoras' enumeration of material ingredients and conditions contribute to our envisioning the "good" or "perfection" of the world, and of the human situation within the world. Anaxagoras does not help us to *understand* at all.

We might expect Socrates to investigate this "best" that he had hoped to find in Anaxagoras' writings. But he does not directly do so. Rather, he emphasizes the role of the mind in interpreting sense data, and introduces hypothetical perfection or ideality as theoretical suppositions whereby human beings orchestrate sensibility.

The sensibility-interpretative-and-organizing role of thinking is emphasized, and simple empiricism is relegated to confusion and senselessness. But this is to say that when human beings thoughtfully organize empirical reality and sense data we do so in terms of *ideas*, the primary function of which, it would seem, is nothing other than this work of sensible organization. It is the organizational function of thinking which allows us to integrate sensibility into coherent patterns,

---

1 Michael Gelven, "Eros and Projection: Plato and Heidegger," From *Thinking About Being: Aspects of Heidegger's Thought*, ed. by Robert W. Shahan and J.W. Mohanty. Copyright © 1984 by the University of Oklahoma Press, p. 128.

and to discuss these patterns without contradiction. And it is the products of the organizing and orchestrating ideas which constitute our respective cultures.

But these organizing ideas—and even more so than in the *Meno,* the much touted Platonic Ideas are here primarily presented in a sensibility-interpretative-and-organizing role—are themselves hypotheses or suppositions which presuppose higher hypotheses in which they are themselves grounded and by which they are themselves organized.

The picture of the working of the human mind that Socrates here offers us is something like the following: human beings interpret and understand sensible experience by organizing it according to ideational hypotheses. But these hypotheses are themselves interpreted and organized by still higher hypotheses. *Et cetera.*

Socrates, of course, encourages his interlocutors to examine their own hypotheses, their own presuppositions, and emphasizes that such an examination proceeds in a two-fold manner. On the one hand and firstly, hypotheses are examined and tested with a view to checking the intelligible coherence of their consequences, the intelligible coherence of the subject-matter organized by them. And then the intellectual schema must be tested with a view to checking its experiential integrity, with a view to checking its coherence with action. Does it work in actual practice? This entails the empirical and experiential testing we have already seen emphasized in the *Meno.* Secondly, hypotheses are examined with a view to uncovering their enrootedness in higher hypotheses or presuppositions. What are the higher hypotheses that ground and support the hypotheses in question? And what do these higher hypotheses themselves presuppose?

The energetic pursuit of such a hierarchical examination would enquire into what I call the direction or orientation of hypothesizing more than into the function or the organizing role of hypothesizing, and in the *Phaedo* it is pursued only as far as a "satisfactory" hypothesis, without further elaboration (101d). The focus here is clearly on what I have called method or procedure, the down-stream organizing-role of hypotheses, and Socrates is content with simply stating that they are up-stream hierarchically organized and integrated as well.

While the up-stream or directional hypothesizing ultimately predominates in Socrates' analysis of knowing—*where* we go is more important than, and even specifies, *how* we go—, the focus of the *Phaedo* is more directed at down-stream, functional hypothesizing. Moral idealizing, that is to say, ultimately predominates—even through such idealizing must be challenged existentially and tested in practice—but it is not here delineated as much as it will be in the *Symposium* and in the *Republic*. It is present, however, and its grounding influence sets the tone of the whole discussion.[1]

But let us not forget the cultural contextualization of the *Phaedo*. Throughout, Plato will throw in asides that clearly indicate that the operative organizing ideas and hypotheses of Socrates' interlocutors are the prevailing cultural ideas and values of Hellas, and which ideas and values they have not clarified and tested. He encourages them to do so, and to conduct their lives in accordance with the words they have exchanged with him in this last and previous conversations. But this is to say that Socrates encourages them to substitute the hypothesizing of Socratic philosophy for the hypothesizing of preceding and prevailing Hellenic culture. And it is also to say that the hypothetical reasoning of Socratic philosophy supplants Pythagorean

---

1 My "up-stream", "down-stream" differentiation is adopted with adaptations from Jacob Needleman, *The Heart of Philosophy* (San Francisco: Harper & Row, 1986).

and preceding Hellenic religion. (Cebes and Simmias are Pythagoreans.)

As his biographical account indicates, Socrates had investigated, clarified and tested the ideational assumptions of the paradigm-contenders of his own day—especially pertaining to the natural philosophy of Anaxagoras. He had greedily grasped at the hints of a "good" interpretation of Nature, only to be thwarted by Anaxagoras' complete refusal to hypothesize any human intellectual and moral good at all. That is to say, the complete elimination of up-stream hypothesizing in Anaxagoras' writings has the effect of proclaiming that his otherwise acceptable down-stream hypothesizing is equivalent to up-stream hypothesizing—a substitution of conditions for *causes*—which Socrates finds totally unacceptable. Socrates, then, is challenged to undertake his own and quite different "second voyage" in search of the cause, in search of the good.

While this "second voyage" is first highlighted in the *Phaedo,* and while, as I have already indicated, its down-stream method and function is there delineated, it is perhaps not incorrect to insist that the *Symposium* is pre-eminently *the* delineation of this "second voyage", pursued now more in terms of direction and orientation, "up-stream", than in terms of the down-stream, methodological procedure of consequential functionalism.

Perhaps more than anything we have seen thus far, the *Symposium* is Plato's *homo-viator*-dissertation, his throwing his hat into the ring of Heraclitean dynamics in a concentrated effort to understand becoming. It is, when all is said and done, a concentrated focusing on where we are going.

And while I have insisted on the distinction between orientation and procedure, I must now acknowledge that one of the conclusions of the *Symposium* is that the two cannot really be separated at all. *Where* we are going and *how* we are going there are ultimately synonymous, and can at best be distinguished only in thought and not in reality. And yet the thoughtful exercise does bring with it advantages. The distinction in thought, then.

The *Symposium* emphatically presents the Beautiful and the Good as the goal towards which human nature is striving. Human beings reach out towards the immortal possession of Beauty and Goodness. Indeed, we *are* such a striving and reaching-out. All mortality *is* a striving after immortality, and human mortality after the immortal possession of Beauty and Goodness.

But we hear very little of this Beauty and Goodness apart from the fact that the eternal possession of it is our specifically human goal, *and that this goal is beyond our reach.* Only the gods, if such there be, eternally possess the Beautiful and the Good. Any description even of Beauty and Goodness lies forever beyond our human capability. We will never "possess" it, we will never even "see" it in such a manner that he could describe it. Rather, Beauty and Goodness is a directional factor indicating *where* we are going, in what direction we are heading. It is decidedly not a statement of a state that we will ever reach.

Human nature is a sign forever pointing beyond itself. It is a perpetually self-overreaching, falling-short-of process. Are we, then, a "useless passion" as Jean-Paul Sartre says?

It seems to me that one of the points that Plato makes in the *Symposium* is precisely that the inevitable failure of human striving does not render this striving senseless or useless. Indeed, this could very well be *the* message that the *Symposium* offers us. Human nature is a passion, yes, and even a *failed* passion. But we are far from being a "useless passion".

The indication of this lies both in the nobility of the *grounding* of this passion that we are and in the exercise of this passion that is available to us as exemplified in the person and behavior of Socrates.

The grounding first. Human nature *is* a response to the Whole. Human nature is summoned by the Transcendent, by Beauty and Goodness. We *are* the Transcendent-summoned, and human life lived properly is a response to Transcendence and therefore noble. The mythic depiction of "recollected" Ideas, especially emphasized in the *Phaedrus* but also found in the *Meno* and the *Phaedo,* is indicative of our Transcendent-summoned nature. I will discuss this in greater detail later when I focus on the Ideas.

The exercise of the proper living of human life. Again, Socrates exemplifies how we can and should live our lives if we want to do so nobly, if we want to be noble human beings. Not-knowing-Socrates, and now the-failed-lover-Socrates, exemplifies the proper exercise of logic- and erotic-behavior, the tragic-response to and the tragic-pursuit of Transcendence.

Diotima's speech to Socrates delineates the stages of the erotic ascent, while emphasizing, remember, that the fourth level, the eternal possession of Beauty, lies forever beyond even his capability. But it is Alcibiades' *encomium* of Socrates which most clearly indicates the concrete and realistic possibilities of noble human behavior. It is one thing to hear Diotima declaim about the four levels of erotic ascent. It is quite another to hear Alcibiades describe very intimately the three-leveled erotic behavior of Socrates. His account of Socrates' response to his attempted seduction, and how the behavior and speech of Socrates makes him ashamed of the morally corrupt life he is living, is a *concrete description of eros in action, eros in deed, rather than simply eros in words.* His account of the physical endurance, martial valor and mystical prowess of Socrates gives us a concrete depiction of the three-tiered erotic-ascensional integrity actually lived by Socrates.

Socrates is eros-incarnate, the new image of cultural and moral excellence offered for our emulation.

Plato ties the many strands of his anthropology and epistemology together in the *Republic*, especially in the three central allegories of the Sun, the Line and the Cave.

What emerges is as follows: responding to the call of Transcendence, human beings construct value-laden/thoughtful interpretations of their world, each of which is dependent upon tradition and yet each aspires to an independent, absolute status.

Human beings are creatures who fabricate interpretations. We are cultural-projecting-creatures who work out of a given interpretative context and project our dependent cultural images and models on the basis of unexamined assumptions, and yet aspire towards an absolute and comprehensive intuition, a presuppositionless and immutable grasp of reality-in-itself.

Interpretative thinking, the distinctively psychic behavior that distinguishes us from other life-forms, operates deductively, drawing conclusions from value-assumptions and hypotheses which are themselves hierarchically arranged so that lower sets of assumptions are dependent upon, suspended from and organized by, higher sets of assumptions. Such a deductive dynamics ensures that it is absolutely impossible that we could ever definitively intuit or unconditionally understand anything. Our knowing is inevitably fallibilistic, value-projective and hypothetically-interpretative. And, like Socrates himself, we are bound to *not*-know absolutely or unconditionally.

What we can do, and what Plato constantly encourages us to do, is gain awareness of our assumption-bound and cultural-bound interpretations. What we can do is examine and test our cultural contexts and the assumptions binding these contexts with respect to their clarity, integrity and viability. What we dare not do is settle down comfortably in our assumption-bound and dependent cultures and claim that we have reality and truth in itself!

Allegorically, humankind is a cave-dwelling creature. Each culture claims that its shadow-drawings projected on the walls of its cave are reality and truth itself. And thereby each culture proclaims that human nature, at bottom, wants reality-and-truth-in-itself and, as it were, is made for reality-and-truth-in-itself.

Now Plato, as we know full well, claims that the possession, and even the perception, of reality-in-itself is forever denied us. The only recourse open to us if we want to be nobly human to the full extent of our power is to examine and test our cultures and assumptions in a passionate and fruitless pursuit of what will remain forever beyond our reach. Far from being a "useless passion", Plato offers it as a model of human excellence that can only be called tragic-comic.

Granted, this is not the usual depiction of Platonic philosophy and its accompanying model of human excellence that has prevailed in our Western cultural tradition. Is this perhaps due to the fact that we, even as Socrates' and Plato's contemporaries, have never been comfortable with admitting our own ignorance? Is it because we, as they, have never been comfortable with admitting that we might not know? Oh, we might very well admit that we individually do not know, and we readily admit that the "others", people of different cultures and religious and political persuasions, certainly do not know. But to claim that absolute and infallible knowledge is entirely beyond the reach of all of us, beyond the reach of Church and Science? Come on!

And yet this is precisely Plato's message! Human beings want to know reality and to possess goodness, unconditionally. We are a great longing and passion to know and possess absolutely. And we inevitably and necessarily fall short of the goal of this longing and passion.

Plato's philosophy, his message to ancient Hellas and to any subsequent peoples and cultures who care to listen is twofold: one, that to be a human being is to be a lover of wisdom, a philosopher; two, that "philosophy" is a tentative working out of the cultural and methodological consequences of a self-conscious appropriation of the reality of not-knowing, of the *loving* of wisdom, of the passion to know and to possess which can never be satisfied.

The delineation of especially the epistemological and logical consequences of this failed-passion which we are remained a preoccupation of Plato's throughout the later dialogues. In these middle dialogues he seems rather satisfied with presenting existential and imagistic depictions of his new culture and morality.

The focal point, of course, is the person and behavior of Socrates. It is absolutely important that we understand that Plato presents an attractive and loving portrait of Socrates in order that his readers might be motivated to imitate him in their own behavior, individually and collectively. Pay attention to *what* Socrates says, but also attend carefully to *how* he says it, to whom he says it, and in what context he says it. Socrates always comes through as concerned, compassionate, kind and loving. His is an all-round human development, and he encourages similar development in his friends. He is not self-centered. He is not vain or greedy. He has no pretensions, and he is committed passionately to the intellectual and moral development of his friends and acquaintances. Witness the interaction between Socrates and Hippocrates in the *Protagoras*. See how he handles Alcibiades in the seduction scene in the *Symposium*. Recall how he addressed his "fellow Athenians" in the *Apology*.

The point of all this is that Plato is well aware of the seductiveness of images—especially images containing contradictory qualities, as do all of the images of Socrates—and is here "working us over" and trying to engender in us an erotic fascination with Socrates so that we will imitate him in our own behavior. Secondly, empirical or experiential testing is operating in these concrete depictions of Socrates. Much was made of experiential testing in the *Meno,* and I claimed that it was much more widely used in the dialogues than is usually admitted. Perhaps the most pervasive use of experiential testing that occurs in these middle dialogues occurs in the concrete and imagistic presentation of the living Socrates existentially instancing the new model of human excellence. Philosophy, erotic-hypothetical thinking, works. Look at Socrates, albeit the dramatically-imaged-Socrates.

But Plato's use of imagery does not stop with depictions of concrete viability. Sensual representation (imagery) pervades these dialogues. The three allegories from the *Republic* spring to mind, as well as the myth of the variegated earth at the end of the *Phaedo.* The ascent to the beautiful in the *Symposium* is highly imagistic. And, of course, the Ideas, of which more shortly, are fundamentally imagistic. And yet there is no denying a basic mistrust of imagery in Plato, and that there is the positing of an ideational thrust designed to transcend images and traffic in "ideas" alone, as it were.

Plato has a love-hate relationship with imagery. On the one hand, he is well aware of the impact and seductive influence that images have on us. Images capture our attention, and, pleasantly presented, can have a decidedly positive and liberating influence upon us. And so he goes to great length to image Socrates positively, and to image positively the laying-down of his hypotheses, the guesses and value-assumptions which organize the cultural message he is trying to launch.

On the other hand, Plato is very conscious of the fascinating and fixating character of imagery. Far too often we become bound-by and locked-into images. Empiricism reigns, and we too readily convince ourselves that reality is in itself the way we perceive it. To counteract this imagistic and sensual closure, Plato will emphasize the transcending and "spiritual" character of thinking. The soul, the power whereby and with which we think, is similarly "spiritualized", and its separation from the body is emphasized.

We do not need to draw *substantial* dualistic conclusions from this. Quite properly, Plato insisted on recognizing a distinction between understanding and perceiving. Human beings not only see, but understand, and there is something supra-sensual and supra-imagistic in our understanding. Plato, at least, was quite convinced that the world is at bottom integrated by *logos* rather than by simple, spatio-temporal, sensual coefficients and images.

So what about Ideas, then? Our tradition has made much of the transcendent-*substantial* status of the Ideas in Plato's philosophy. As a consequence, we have emphasized a two-world dualism, a world of Being and a world of Becoming, a world of intelligibility and spirit and a world of sensibility and matter. There is no doubt but that such words and distinctions are Platonic. What is doubtful, however, is that Plato taught a literal-and-substantial understanding of these words and distinctions. Whereas Plato contested a substantial dualism in his own culture, we have ignored the irony of his own writings and made him a spokesman for that very irrationality which he opposed.

Hellenic poetic mythology and especially Pythagorean religion claimed to know the ultimate, metaphysical structure of reality. This reality, according to Plato's contemporaries, the Pythagoreans, was divided into two "worlds", into the world of being and spirit and the world of becoming and matter. Human beings are sojourners in this life of becoming, and our true home lies in the after-life in the world of being and spirit which we shall reach if we follow the true knowledge and practices of Pythagoreanism.

Later, Christianity loved this religious philosophy, pruned it of its "excesses", and handed it down as Platonism and part and parcel of its own philosophical and dualistic explanation of life.

But it is not Plato at all. Plato is firmly focused on Socratic not-knowing, and he determinedly fought all pretensions-to-knowing which deviated from this new model of human excellence.

But the Platonic myths are Pythagorean. Of course they are. And in each and every instance Plato takes great care to indicate that his myths are myths, "likely stories", and are not to be literally accepted as apodictic, factual delineations of reality. Do we read Plato carefully enough to detect this? And if not, why not?

The traditional metaphysical dualism is not entirely wide of the mark, however. It is fallacious and damaging in its substantial and infallibilistic claims, I think, but it is most certainly correct in its insistence on an ignorance vs. knowledge and darkness vs. light distinction.

Plato's central message is the challenge that human beings liberate themselves from ignorance and darkness through thinking and loving, through the exercise of erotic-hypothetical reasoning, through *Logos*. Human excellence and "liberation" lies along this path, and in the "upper reaches" of this path. Most certainly. But we have deceived ourselves into thinking that such *Logos* entails a claim to knowledge. We have deceived ourselves into thinking that not-knowing and knowing can be "located" in substantially and entitatively distinct "worlds". And in the process we have promoted irresponsibility towards the spatio-temporal world of lived experience, putting all of our effort into attaining the "heavenly world" of Ideas only after death.

But Plato's world is entitatively one. It is the world of human experience, encompassing the full range of phenomena and dispositions which we find about us. It is the human situation and circumstance, in the full range of its factual and possible ramifications. The world is multi-tendential, a mixture of things and activities at once chaotic and unorganized and at the same time coherent and organized.

The chaotic world Plato refers to as matter and sensibility. Contentment with such, and with such as it is represented in the traditional and contemporary cultures against which Socrates contended, is beneath human dignity. The specifically human world, the world towards which we struggle and towards which we are the struggle, is an intelligibly organized and coherent world. It is a cosmos that supports a viable, intelligently coherent and morally beautiful and good political structure.

By intelligent and moral organization I refer to what seems to have been Plato's belief that reality was intelligible, was a hierarchical organization of conditioned patterns and relationships suspended from a perfectly good, intelligible and unconditioned source, variously referred to as the One, and the Beautiful and the Good.

Human beings are the passion to perceive this absolute and unconditioned source which forever lies beyond their reach. We are this infinite passion which forever falls short of itself. We are this passion for the Absolute and Transcendent which forever dances just beyond our outstretched arms. But we reach out nonetheless, responding to the alluring appeal of the Absolute itself by forming idea-hypotheses in the self-transcending dynamism of the erotic-logic of thinking and loving. Ideas are the hypotheses we form, the intelligent guesses we fabricate as we endlessly struggle, responding to the Transcendent Whole, to clarify and organize our world.

The "sneak-previewing" of the Ideas in the *Phaedrus* is perhaps relevant here. Much has been made of the sharply-drawn illustration of the winged soul, and of the and winged horses comprising it.

Indeed, it is a beautiful tale, and the account of the human souls peering over the edge of the universe itself and viewing the Ideas is positively rapturous. But it is a tale and a metaphor for all that. Metaphor can bespeak truth, however, albeit indirectly. And the truth that this metaphor bespeaks is clearly articulated by Plato as follows:

> For only the soul that has beheld truth may enter into this our human form—seeing that man must understand the language of forms, passing from a plurality of perceptions to a unity gathered together by reasoning... *Phaedrus* 249 b-c[1]

That is to say, it is an essential characteristic of human minds that they utilize Forms or Ideas as hypothetically integrative and orchestrating patternings of existentiality. The human mind understands, and it understands by laying-down Ideas as hypotheses. Ideas *are* hypotheses. They are world-organizing, culture-creating existential hypotheses.

Plato must be seen as a passionate pursuer of *Logos,* and indeed as a passionate transformer of *Mythos* into *Logos*. Yes. Under his attention the traditional Homeric myths are demythologized and rationalized. And in a very real sense the whole of Platonic philosophy can be seen as a demythologization and rationalization of Pythagorean myth. Yes. Plato will annoy and badger poetry and traditional mythology because it does not know and understand that of which it speaks. It cannot clearly articulate and speak its message. But to be a human being is to be a speaker, and clear speech, *Logos,* must reign supreme in human culture. Plato therefore will ban poetry and

---

1 *The Collected Dialogues of Plato, op. cit.*

he will demythologize myth in his passion for philosophy and Logos. Yes, all of this is quite true and very important indeed.

But it is not the whole truth, and were we to stop with it, it would become a very superficial and fundamentally anti-Platonic 'truth'. *Logos* is mythos-dependent, and the final word in Plato's passionate pursuit of *Logos* is *Mythos*!

I have argued above that erotic-hypothesizing is the logic of Plato's new culture, of his new image and model of human excellence. Here I want to state simply that erotic-hypothesizing is *Logos*. *Logos is* erotic-hypothesizing.

Do not be confused by the multiplicity of terms. Unlike some contemporary logical and positive thinkers, Plato insisted that terms are indices, signs pointing towards meanings which we can never fully grasp. And he does not hesitate to use different terms, different words, to point towards single meanings. *Logos* and Hypothesis are synonyms.

By and large the two are not synonymous for us because we understand logic differently than Plato did. For us logic connotes necessary inference and eternal validity. Logic is the science of deductive reasoning which, properly conducted, conveys absolute and infallible, albeit, perhaps, merely formal knowledge.

But this is not Plato's *Logos* for at least two reasons: one, absolute and infallible knowledge is forever beyond the legitimate claim of human beings or of any human science, and two, Platonic *Logos* is two-directional, deductive and 'inductive', and the former is dependent upon the latter.

I don't like the term "inductive" in the former statement and have therefore placed it in single quotation marks. The contemporary connotation of "induction" is quite removed, I think, from the up-stream directional analysis that Plato utilizes in the allegory of the

Line, and other places. You recall the differently directed analyses of level three thinking and level four thinking in the aforementioned allegory? Level three thinking or *Logos* consisted of deducing conclusions from unexamined assumptions/hypotheses. Level four *Logos*, proceeding in exactly the opposite direction, sought to ground hypotheses in an unhypothetical, presuppositionless beginning.

We know, of course, what comes of this venture.

But the point of all this is that deductive or descensional logic is grounded in inductive or ascensional logic, in hypothesizing literally understood (*Republic* 511b). Down-stream hypothesizing is grounded in up-stream hypothesizing. That is to say, *Logos* is grounded in, suspended from, *Mythos*, in guesses that organize phenomena.

Myth, accordingly, plays a much more intensive and extensive role in the Platonic dialogues and philosophy than is usually recognized. And I'm not just talking about the more colorful myths such as the Variegated Earth and the Winged Soul. The central myth of Platonic philosophy is humanity's passionate, frustrated hypothetical pursuit of Beauty and Goodness in response to the appeal of this Beauty and Goodness itself. The central myth is Erotic-Hypothesizing, *Logos* itself.

Plato's philosophy, and his message to his contemporaries and subsequent generations, is but his attempt to rationalize this myth without destroying it. And we can destroy it in two ways, it seems to me. One, we can deny outright that the human world and reality itself is grounded in Intelligibility, Beauty and Goodness. Then we would have turned away from Plato, and so far as Plato is concerned, we would have turned away from our very humanity itself. Two, we can claim absolute certitude and infallibility; we can claim that we, at least, know that we have the truth. Again, we would have turned away from Plato and we would have denied our very humanity. Socrates, remember, does not know. Knowledge is perhaps the lot of the gods. It is never the lot of human beings.

But why not turn away from Plato? Why not claim that chaos and irrationality ground and inevitably characterize the human world and reality itself? Why not claim that "might is right", and that any moral characterization of "right" and "good" and "truth" have nothing to do with the human lot anyway? Or, finally, why not claim that I and mine are good and right and we will crush anyone or anything that stands in our way? Why not indeed?

The answer, of course, is that such claims just do not work. We have made precisely these claims in the last two thousand years of our Western culture. And it is perhaps our having turned away from *Logos*-as-delineated-by-Plato which has landed us in the mess in which we find ourselves today.

It is not, then, a question of turning back to Plato, so much as it is a question of turning to him for the first time! But this is not even true. For, nurtured as we are by a culture grounded however faithlessly in Plato, we cannot escape the call that he directs at us and the pressure he exerts upon us. Like the prisoners in his Cave, we are bathed in his summoning light, and we are constantly called-forth, eternally called-forth to the not knowing of Erotic-*Logos*. Our return, inevitably, is an eternal return.

But I'm not sure we are ready for such an eternal return just yet. In fact, I'm not sure we will ever be ready for it! You see, Plato is one of the first and still very few thinkers who consciously and conscientiously tried to come to grips with the reality of not-knowing. And his conclusion that echoes down through history and challenges us, our culture and our institutions is that no one knows, no one ever knows absolutely and unconditionally. At best, we desire knowledge. And when we are living at the peak of our humanity, when we are doing our best, we are seekers after knowledge, we are philosophers, forever reaching out towards truth and reality and forever falling short of grasping it and possessing it.

And now let me conclude this rambling Interpretation with a few words about the style and structure of the dialogues themselves.

It is no accident that Plato did not write textbooks and didactic pieces. To have done so he would have had to know; he would have had to possess a body of information systematically organized which was true and which definitively answered the relevant questions. But this is precisely what the early and middle period Plato does not possess, or at least this is what his main character, Socrates, constantly tells us. Human beings do *not* know. Socrates does not have *answers*. We do not *possess* the *truth*.

Plato certainly has a message he wishes to communicate to us, and it is precisely what I have written in the above paragraph: We do not know, so let's poke around and see what we can find. We do not have answers, so let's see if we can ask some interesting questions. We do not possess the truth, so let's get together and see if we can come up with some guesses and hypotheses that might just open up new possibilities for us.

There is another reason why Plato did not give us any answers, and in the long run this might be one of the more frightening messages he offers us: Plato doesn't give us any answers because he wants us to come up with our own. Not exactly. Remember that for Plato there are no answers anyway. No, *Plato wants us to think,* and he wants us to think on our own—the only way, after all, that thinking can be done.

Remember, Plato is trying to transform an existing culture; he is trying to fabricate a new model of human excellence. He is trying to draw up a picture of human beings as *thinking* animals.

Plato wants us to think. Now how do you get someone to think? Quite obviously, you demonstrate it, show it to them, and then you "con" them into it. And this is precisely what Plato tries to do in his dialogues. First of all, he paints a very attractive and seductive image of Socrates. He is a lovable old thinker. He is lovable and therefore he is imitable. And that is exactly what Plato wants each of us to think and to do. Look carefully at what Socrates does, for Socrates demonstrates how one should think and love. But the demonstrations are never air-tight. Inevitably questions arise and further delineations are called for, and we feel ourselves drawn into the very questioning and thinking that is called for. And this is exactly what Plato wants.

But is it true? Is *Logos* and erotic-hypothesizing the essence of humanity?

I don't know. Plato paints a nice picture, and I suppose that in the last analysis Platonic philosophizing must be seen as artistic creativity. Erotic-hypothesizing is, ultimately, interpretation. And interpretation is art, poesis. In the last analysis, then, Plato journeyed through myth to logic to poetry. To be a human being is to be a poet. But is it true?

CONCLUDING REMARKS

In my Interpretation I stated that we were entering an era in which, for the first time, we would be able to hear the Socratic message. Surely, in a purportedly philosophical treatise such a statement sounds silly. Ability, possibility is always available to us.

Yes, of course. But then such a "pure" possibility reveals one of the perennial characteristics which has accompanied our very un-Socratic Western philosophy thus far. Pure possibility is, of course, always possible "purely" (whatever that might mean) and abstractly, but it is an abstract and theoretical character which has no necessary connection whatsoever to actuality. Pure possibility implies dualism, and is quite removed from the existentially political concerns of Socrates and Plato.

Historically we have made a substantial Idealism out of Plato's philosophy, and not a few of us have wondered why it did not work in the existential and socio-political world in which we were caught up. Such schizophrenic chasing after shadows could go on forever.

It could, I say, in the abstract and dualistic world of Idealism. In the existing world of lived experience, however, it could not go on forever precisely because of the discordant parameters introduced into lived experience by the very dogmatic logic which had fuelled its successful development. This development is self-annihilating and self-destructive. The evidence of this is all about us today. And it is this very evidence of the unviability of (dogmatic) knowledge and power which is offering us the real possibility of hearing Socrates' message today for the very first time.

But being able to hear is no guarantee that we will actually begin to listen. Surely, one of the tenets of Socratic philosophizing is that no one person can teach anyone else anything at all. Oh, we can learn from others. Yes, indeed. But then we must *want* to learn, we must reach out towards knowing in full consciousness of our own not-knowing.

Do we, then, want to learn? Do we want to know? Do we want to continue on the path trod by Anytos and Meletos, or like the slave-boy do we now want to recognize that we do not know and, grounded on the reflective appropriation of our not-knowing, set about examining ourselves, our prejudices and our priorities? Hopefully, the massive difficulties which our very knowledge showers upon us today will prompt us to recognize our fundamental *not* knowing, and we will then want to learn and want to know.

When that happens, Plato will have already painted for us in very broad strokes the logic we will follow in our pursuit. And this *Logos* of erotic-hypothesizing I have tried to delineate.

Erotic-hypothesizing is a myth. And it is situated within a much larger myth, variously depicted in the Dialogues, which animates and grounds the myth of *Logos* or erotic-hypothesizing itself—perhaps it would be better to say *evokes* the myth of *Logos* or erotic-hypothesizing.

In my Introduction, I said that our Christian heritage believes that human beings are implicated within a good and intelligible whole which calls them towards itself. As well as being Hebraic, this belief is decidedly Platonic. The world is good, beautiful and intelligible for

Plato. By all means. But, if I might use some Aristotelian terminology—the meaning of which Aristotle took from Plato anyway—the world is only *potentially* so, and it calls to human beings to *actualize* it. We engage in this actualization process by ascending the stages of erotic-hypothesizing as depicted in the allegories of the Line, the Cave and ascent to the Beautiful.

The basic metaphysical or ontological structure of this myth is what we might perhaps call Appeal-Response dialectics. Transcendence *appeals* to the human consciousness, the human "soul", and the noble man or woman, the imitator of Socrates, *responds* by striving to understand and possess the Whole. Of course we fail. The Whole dances-forever just beyond our reach, calling us above and beyond ourselves in the perpetual self-transcending that constitutes Human Excellence.

And let us not forget Plato's commitment to political engagement, the forceful (if necessary) return of the liberated prisoner to the cave. Knowing and loving is a hierarchical conformation to the beautiful, good and intelligible Whole that necessarily expresses itself in existential and political activity. The lover of wisdom (philosopher) reigns, if not in today's narrow sense of politics, then in ennobling creativity that raises the standard of excellence in the human community, in the *Polis*.

Humanity *is* a response to Transcendence. Human intelligence and human erotic behavior *is* a response to Transcendence. The human soul has viewed the Ideas and harbors the memory of them within itself, Plato poetically insists. But our proper and right response to the appeal from Transcendence constantly calling to us is by no means guaranteed. We can 'turn away' from Transcendence and fixate ourselves in the fascinations of immanence. We can deny our own not-knowing and arrogantly parade the grandeur of 'knowledge'. We can follow Alcibiades rather than Socrates.

What, then, might be the practical consequences of a turning to Plato and of a listening to Socrates for perhaps the first time? I don't know. But I should imagine that our imitating Socrates and attuning ourselves to a Good, Beautiful and Intelligible Whole which dances forever just beyond our reach should translate itself into much more pacific practices, and into much more humane and long-term viable practices than has been our habit to date.

It is only fitting that Plato have the last word:

> Then supposing you should ever hence-forth try to conceive afresh, Theaetetus, if you succeed, your embryo thoughts will be better as a consequence of today's scrutiny, and if you remain barren, you will be gentler and more agreeable to your companions, having the good sense not to fancy you know what you do not know. *Theaetetus* 210c[1]

---

1 *The Collected Dialogues, op. cit.*

BIBLIOGRAPHY

PRIMARY WORKS CITED:

The Great Dialogues of Plato, trans. by W.H.D. Rouse, edited by Eric. H. Warmington and Philip G. Rouse (New York: New American Library, 1956).

The Collected Dialogues of Plato, Including the Letters, edited by Edith Hamilton and Huntington Cairns (Princeton, New Jersey: Princeton University Press, 1963).

SECONDARY WORKS CITED:

Kenneth Dorter, *Plato's Phaedo, An Interpretation* (Toronto: University of Toronto Press, 1982).

Julius Elias, *Plato's Defense of Poetry* (London: Macmillan Press, 1984).

Michael Gelven, "Eros and Projection: Plato and Heidegger, "*Thinking About Being: Aspects of Heidegger's Thought,* edited by R.W. Shahan and S.N. Mohanty (Norman: University of Oklahoma Press, 1984).

Alexandre Koyré, *Discovering Plato* (New York: Columbia University Press, 1945).

Raoul Naroll, "The Logic of Generalization", *A Handbook of Method in Cultural Anthropology,* edited by Raoul Naroll and Ronald Cohen (New York and London: Columbia University Press, 1973).

Jacob Needleman, *The Heart of Philosophy* (San Francisco: Harper and Row, 1986).

Mary P. Nichols, *Socrates and the Political Community, An Ancient Debate* (Albany: State University of New York Press, 1987).

Friedrich Nietzsche, *Twilight of the Idols, The Portable Nietzsche,* edited by Walter Kaufmann (Penguin Books, 1977).

John Herman Randall, Jr., *Plato, Dramatist of the Life of Reason* (New York and London: Columbia University Press, 1970).

J.E. Raven, *Plato's Thought in the Making* (Cambridge: Cambridge University Press, 1965).

John Sallis, *Being and Logos, The Way of Platonic Dialogue* (Pittsburgh: Duquesne University Press, 1975).

Thomas G. West, *Plato's Apology of Socrates, an interpretation with a new translation* (Ithaca and London: Cornell University Press, 1979).

SECONDARY WORKS CONSULTED:

Borna Bebek, *The Third City, Philosophy at war with positivism* (London: Routledge and Kegan Paul, 1982).

James Bechman, *The Religious Dimension of Socrates' Thought* (Waterloo, Ontario: Wilfrid Laurier University Press, Canadian Corporation for Studies in Religion, 1979).

R.H.S. Crossman, *Plato Today* (London: Unwin, 1971).

Robert E. Cushman, *Therapeia, Plato's Conception of Philosophy* (Westport, Conn.: Greenwood Press, 1976).

Hans-Georg Gadamer, *Dialogue and Dialectic: Eight Hermeneutical Studies on Plato,* translated and with and Introduction by P. Christopher Smith (New Haven and London: Yale University Press, 1980).

Charles L. Griswold, Jr., *Self-knowledge in Plato's Phaedrus* (New Haven: Yale University Press, 1986).

Eric A. Havelock, *Preface to Plato* (Cambridge, Mass.: Harvard University Press, 1963).

Werner Jaeger, *Paideia: the Ideals of Greek Culture,* translated from the second German Edition by Gilbert Highet (New York: Oxford University Press, 1962).

Sir David Ross, *Plato's Theory of Ideas* (Oxford: Clarendon Press, 1951).

Gilbert Ryle, *Plato's Progress* (Cambridge: Cambridge University Press, 1966).

Kenneth M. Sayre, *Plato's Late Ontology, A Riddle Resolved* (Princeton, New Jersey: Princeton University Press, 1982).

Leo Strauss, *The City and Man* (Chicago and London: The University of Chicago Press, 1978).

A.E. Taylor, *Socrates, the Man and His Thought* (New York: Doubleday Anchor Books).

A.E. Taylor, *The Mind of Plato* (Ann Arbour: Ann Arbour Paperbacks, The University of Michigan Press, 1960).

Henry Teloh, *The Development of Plato's Metaphysics* (University Park and London: the Pennsylvania State University Press, 1981).

Laszlo Versenyi, *Socratic Humanism* (New Haven and London: Yale University Press, 1963).

The Philosophy of Socrates, edited by Gregory Vlastos (Notre Dame: University of Notre Dame Press, 1980).

Plato, A Collection of Critical Essays I: Metaphysics and Epistemology, edited by Gregory Vlastos (New York: Anchor Books, 1971).

Plato, A Collection of Critical Essays II: Ethics, Politics, and Philosophy of Art and Religion, edited by Gregory Vlastos (Notre Dame: University of Notre Dame Press, 1978).

John Wild, *Plato's Modern Enemies and the Theory of Natural Law* (Chicago and London: The University of Chicago Press, 1953).

INDEX